WOMEN WHO KEPT THE LIGHTS

An Illustrated History of Female Lighthouse Keepers

Mary Louise Clifford
J. Candace Clifford

Cypress Communications
Williamsburg, Virginia
1993

Printed in the United States of America by Data Reproductions Corporation

10 9 8 7 6 5

Library of Congress Catalog Card Number 93-74066

ISBN 0-963-64120-4

Front cover: *The Tabberrah family at Cumberland Head Light around 1880. This light was kept by Emma Tabberrah from 1904 until 1919. The station is now a private residence. Photo made from a tintype belonging to Arthur B. Hillegas.*

Back cover: *Blackistone Island Light on the Potomac River, kept by Josephine Freeman from 1876 until 1912. This station no longer exists. Courtesy of The Mariners' Museum, Newport News, Virginia.*

Designed, produced, and published by Cypress Communications, Williamsburg, Virginia

Table of Contents

List of Sidebars

Acknowledgments

Piecing together *Women Who Kept the Lights* was very much like doing a jigsaw puzzle. Some of the pieces are still missing, but a great many generous people helped to provide the pieces that are assembled here.

The search began at the National Archives in Washington, where Archivist Angie S. Vandereedt was very helpful in acquainting us with Record Group 26, which contains extensive lighthouse material. At the Suitland Reference Branch of the National Archives James Cassedy produced many of the original lighthouse logs kept by women and copied requested pages for us.

Letters were written to every imaginable source that might have connections with each lighthouse on our list. A number of recipients—among them staff at national and state parks, wildlife refuges, state historic preservation offices, and state historical societies—suggested other places to look. Although their names are too numerous to mention, their suggestions were valuable and appreciated.

We are grateful to Sue Lemmon, historian at Mare Island Naval Shipyard, for steering us to Carolyn Curtain in Williamsburg, Virginia, who shared her recollections of her grandmother Kate McDougal's life at Mare Island Light, California. Mrs. Joseph Church of Plattsburgh, New York, led us to Arthur B. Hillegas of New Baltimore, Michigan, who shared his memories of his grandmother Emma Tabberrah at Cumberland Head Light, New York, and also sent family photos. Finding both of these descendants was like finding precious gems. John Sculley, town historian of Plattsburgh provided a copy of the town seal which is adorned with the Cumberland Head Light.

Other responses provided pieces to the puzzle, and soon made it apparent that generally women keepers who had long careers found a place in the written records. Peggy M. Timlin, curator of manuscripts and books for the Pilgrim Society in Plymouth, corrected misinformation about Hannah Thomas at Gurnet Point Light, Massachusetts. Charles Brilvitch, historian of the City of Bridgeport, provided articles about Kate Moore at Black Rock Light in Connecticut and directed us to Mary Witowski, head of historical collections at the Bridgeport Public Library for photos and citations.

Barbara Swartz, deputy mayor of the Village of Old Field, sent information about Elizabeth Smith and Mary Foster at Old Field Point Light, New York. Tim Wallis, curator of historic facilities at the Tullis-Toledano Manor in Biloxi, Mississippi, sent clippings and articles about the three women who kept the Biloxi Light. Murella Hebert Powell, local history and genealogy librarian at the Biloxi Public Library, provided additional clippings and a photo of Miranda Younghans.

Lynn S. Beman, executive director at the Hudson River Maritime Museum, sent clippings and fact sheets about and photographs of Catherine Murdock at Rondout Point Light, New York. Patricia Harris and John Reed, successive curators at the Old Lighthouse Museum in Michigan City, provided extensive material about Harriet Colfax at Michigan City Light, Indiana.

Michael Redmon, librarian of the Santa Barbara Historical Society, sent photos of Julia Williams at Santa Barbara Light, California. Luther Barrett, trustee of the Delta County Historical Society, passed on what he had learned about Mary Terry at Sand Point Light, Michigan. Melissa Pagano, park and recreation aide at Stony Point Battlefield, sent clippings and a short biography of Nancy Rose at Stony Point Light, New York. Rachel Brett Harley and Betty MacDowell, directors of the History of Michigan Women Project, sent information on Elizabeth Williams at Beaver Point Harbor Light and on two more obscure women who kept Michigan lights. Valuable additional material and photos of Elizabeth Williams at Beaver Point came from Shirley G. Gladish, director of the Beaver Island Historical Society. Ed Deci at the Monhegan Historical and Cultural Museum Association provided vital statistics on Betsy G. Humphrey at Monhegan Light in Maine.

Richard J. Dodds, curator of maritime history at Calvert Marine Museum, sent correspondence pertaining to Josephine Freeman at Blakistone Island Light, Maryland. Dr. Elaine Epps of the Maryland Division of Historical and Cultural Programs added information on Maryland lights. Helen Allen, director/curator of the Clinton County Historical Association, provided information on Emma Tabberrah at Cumberland Head Light and Mary J. Herwerth at Bluff Point Light, both on Lake Champlain in New York. Elinor A. De Wire sent useful suggestions and an article about Kate Marvin at Squaw Point Light, Michigan. Lorena M. Guzman, secretary of the Friends of Concord Point Lighthouse, sent a brochure. Sally Legakis, registrar of Santa Cruz City Museum of Natural History, provided a long article about and photos of Laura Hecox at Santa Cruz Light, California. Sincere thanks to all these individuals for sharing their resources.

As a docent at the Point Pinos Light in California, Clifford Gallant set about collecting information on women lighthouse keepers more than a decade ago. He wrote several articles derived from his research, but never put together the book he planned. His widow gave his files to the U.S. Lighthouse Society in San Francisco, and has our appreciation for doing so. Those files and Clifford Gallant's articles provided information about Catherine Moore at Black Rock Light, Connecticut; Ann David at Point Lookout Light, Maryland; Barbara Mabrity at Key West Light, Florida; Charlotte Layton and Emily Fish at Point Pinos Light, California; Kate Walker at Robbins Reef Light, New York; and Margaret Norvell at Port Pontchartrain Light, Louisiana. We thank Tanja Rabbitt and Wayne Wheeler for their help and hospitality during our visit to the U.S. Lighthouse Society headquarters.

The files of the U.S. Coast Guard Historian's Office in Washington, D.C., provided information about Ida Lewis at Lime Rock Light, Rhode Island, and Fannie Salter at Turkey Point Light, Maryland. Coast Guard historians Kevin Foster and Robert Browning were very helpful in locating materials.

The Mariners' Museum in Newport News, Virginia, was a source of information about and photos of Fannie Salter and Turkey Point Light. Fannie's daughter, Olga Salter Crouch, still living in North East, Maryland, identified family members in Turkey Point photos.

Susannah Livingston's meticulous review contributed to the quality of this manuscript. We are grateful for the interest and assistance of all the many individuals who have responded to our requests for help.

The first lighthouse in the American colonies, Boston Light was built on Little Brewster Island in Boston Harbor in 1716. A tax on all vessels using the harbor paid for maintaining the light. Boston Light was one of 12 colonial lighthouses that came under federal ownership after the War for Independence, and is the only lighthouse in the United States that still has a keeper on site today. Courtesy of the National Archives, #26-LG-5-55.

I. Introduction

The first woman known to keep a lighthouse in America—
Hannah Thomas—lived with her husband at the end of a long
narrow spit of land that forms the protective northern arm
around Plymouth harbor. Local records tell us that the
lighthouse with its twin lanterns was built in 1768 on land
belonging to John Thomas. Massachusetts Bay Colony paid him
rent of five shillings for his land and £200 a year to act as keeper.
In 1776 John Thomas joined a Massachusetts regiment and went
off to fight the British, leaving Hannah to tend the lights on
Gurnet Point.

Very little is known of Hannah Thomas's experiences in that
isolated spot through the long years of the War for
Independence. She must have been lonely and occasionally
frightened. Certainly the responsibility of keeping the lamps
burning night after night after night as hostile British frigates
cruised up and down the coast was unrelenting. We can only
assume that she met the challenge.

When the colonies formed the United States, Gurnet Point
was one of the 12 existing lighthouses that came under federal
ownership and became the responsibility of the Treasury
Department. Twelve more were built on the Atlantic Coast by
the turn of the century.

Lighthouse keepers in the 18th and 19th centuries, male
and female, faced much danger and performed heavy physical
labor. Ida Lewis at Lime Rock Light, Kate Walker at Robbins
Reef Light, and Margaret Norvell at Port Pontchartrain Light
(there may have been others we do not know about) launched
wooden dinghies to make daring rescues of shipwrecked
mariners. In 1846 Rebecca Flaherty (who in 1830 had taken
over her husband John's duties as keeper of the Sand Key Light
in the Florida Keys) and her five children drowned in a hurricane
when the tower in which they had taken refuge was swept away.
Several women keepers—Abbie Burgess at Matinicus Rock

Light, Maria Younghans at Biloxi Light, Barbara Mabrity at Key West Light, and Harriet Colfax at Michigan City Light—are known to have stayed at their posts to keep the lights burning through terrifying storms and hurricanes.

In the 19th century, lighthouse keeping was very much a family affair, and the lighthouse service made use of the free labor families could provide. Keepers were often responsible for tending minor lights, which took them away from their station. They were permitted to pursue other jobs, such as fishing or piloting ships into harbors or farming. Members of their families, including wives and daughters, learned to keep the lights burning when their men were away. When a male keeper fell ill or died, many of these women simply took over their husband's or father's duties, often receiving official appointments because there was no pension system to care for them. The fifth auditor of the Treasury Department, Stephen Pleasonton, responsible for the lighthouse service from 1820 to 1852, was comfortable with appointing women keepers, and felt that widows and daughters of keepers were particularly worthy candidates for their positions.

This auditor also saw to it that appointments of new keepers were systematically recorded after 1828. No complete record of keepers' names before that date exists. Any attempt to peer back into history and summon up the women who might have been keeping lighthouses at the turn of that century is obscured by the gaps in the historical records, reflecting the lack of interest in recording the accomplishments of working men and women in that period. After 1828 "Lighthouse Keepers and Assistants" in the National Archives—seven hand-written ledgers which served as the official record of lighthouse keeper appointments and salaries between 1828 and 1905—reveals the names of at least 122 women who were appointed official keepers in their own name. Twice that number were officially appointed assistant keepers, generally aiding their fathers or husbands. A great many more women never received official appointments, but kept a light for a few months after a husband's death—until a new keeper arrived at the station.

The exploits of these women have not been recorded in places where the public can become familiar with them. Much of the published literature about women in the 19th century focused on prescriptions for proper female behavior, expressing social norms formulated largely by men. Their writings described the ideal female, emphasizing the passivity of her nature and her domestic attributes, and focused on middle- and upper-class, white, northern, urban women. The actual experiences of women who were forced by circumstances to earn their own living, of immigrant women, and of black women bore no relation to those established norms.[1]

Because writers of the time did not feel that the activities of working women were exemplary, very few noted their accomplishments. Actually, the same can be said for blue-collar working men. Not until the 20th century do we find male lighthouse keepers sharing their personal experiences on the job. The men and women who kept the lights were, by and large, not drawn from a class that recorded their activities. Only when newspaper journalists picked up the drama of fierce storms or perilous rescues or unusual careers were the exploits of either sex made a matter of permanent record.

The written record is far more complete regarding the construction and maintenance of the light stations because of annual reports published after the Civil War by the Lighthouse Board and periodic reports about the conditions at the stations by the inspectors who regularly visited the light stations. Other than the appointment records and the 10-year census, lighthouse keepers become known mainly through secondary sources—obituaries and newspaper articles focused on dramatic episodes or unusually long careers. Personal histories may have been handed down orally within families, but those are largely lost to us now.

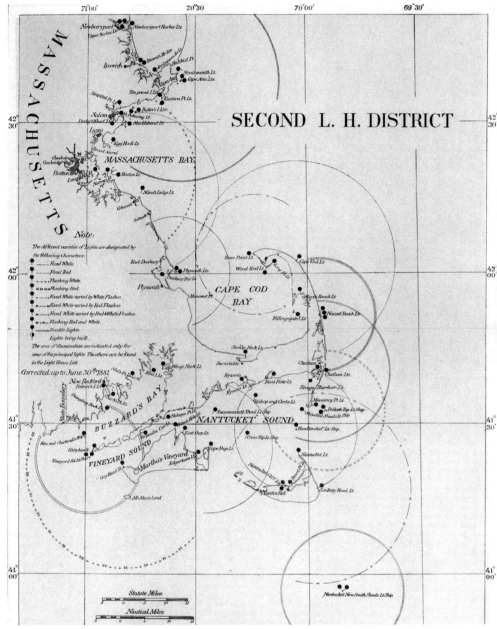

Maps showing light station locations according to the districts of the period are taken from the 1881 Annual Report of the Lighthouse Board. *The 13 maps in the report show 590 light stations in the United States. In 1881 at least 21 of these had officially appointed female keepers, or 3.5 percent of the total.*

II. Hannah Thomas at Gurnet Point Light, Massachusetts, 1776-1786

What is actually known about Hannah Thomas could be related in a sentence or two because the records are so scanty. Her story can only be fleshed out by reciting the history of her time and what is known about her lighthouse.

The first lighthouse at Gurnet Point was erected in 1768. The structure was 30 feet long, 15 feet wide, and 20 feet high, with a lantern on each end containing two lamps in each, the first American "twin lights." The lanterns, which protected the lamps against the weather, were constructed of heavy wooden frames holding small, thick panes of glass. These twin lanterns, were easily distinguishable from nearby Barnstable Light, and could be lined up by mariners, giving an exact location at that one point.

In Hannah's era the lighthouse keeper's job was a seven-day-a-week responsibility. The two lamps in each lantern at Gurnet Point had to be lit and kept burning every night of the week, every day of the year. When Hannah took charge, the tallow candles used in the earliest lanterns in the colonies had been abandoned, for their light was too feeble to be visible from any distance. She tended four flat-wick lamps (also called bucket lamps) without any reflecting apparatus, each having four large wicks.

The lamps burned whale oil, which gave off a large amount of smoke and soot, dimming the light and hazing over the glass around the lantern. Hannah had to replenish the oil in the lamps two or three times during the night, trim the wicks, and wipe the glass clean. At dawn, she extinguished the lamps and cleaned them.

The American colonists were very dependent on the sea, not only for traveling from place to place, but for fish to eat and for transporting supplies and manufactured goods along the coast and to and from Europe. Ship captains had such a dire need for landmarks, both in daylight and darkness, to tell them their location and guide them into safe havens along our coasts and waterways, that they paid harbor fees to finance lighthouses or launched lotteries to raise the necessary money to erect them.

The colonists who declared independence in 1776 had no navy—a disadvantage from which they suffered throughout the Revolutionary War. Sailing ships of the British Navy, armed with cannon, prowled up and down the coast to harass, give chase to, and capture unarmed commercial vessels whenever they found them. The calculating eyes of British naval commanders must have studied the lonely lighthouses which marked the hazards and harbors along the Atlantic Coast. If those landmarks could be put out of commission, or better still, destroyed, then the commercial ships of the rebellious colonists would be far more vulnerable to British attack.

Nineteenth century twin towers at Gurnet Point in Plymouth Harbor. When John Thomas went off to war in 1776, his wife Hannah carried on his duties from 1776 until 1786. Courtesy of the National Archives, #26-LG-7-11.

Hannah Thomas

The residents of the three small towns on Plymouth Bay—Plymouth, Duxbury, and Kingston—knew that the lights at Gurnet Point were in danger, and so they threw up earthworks and built a crude fort around the lighthouse to protect it from the guns of British ships. How great a sense of security would this have given Hannah Thomas as she went about her daily duties?

Hannah would certainly have watched with dismay when in 1778 the British frigate *Niger*, maneuvering just offshore, went aground on the shoals of Brown's Bank. In the gun battle between the stranded frigate and the colonists defending Gurnet Point, a wild shot from the ship pierced the walls of Hannah's lighthouse, but the lights in the twin lanterns at either end of the building were not damaged. Repairs to Hannah's dwelling were not made until 1783, two years after the war ended.

A "History of Plymouth (Gurnet) Light, Massachusetts" (author and source unknown) on file in the National Archives states that "in 1778 the armed brigantine *General Arnold* was caught in a blizzard while less than a mile from the light and the captain anchored his vessel rather than risk the treacherous water of Plymouth's inner harbor without a pilot. The vessel dragged anchor and hit on White Flats. Seventy-two of the crew died, most of them freezing to death in the below-zero temperature before they could be rescued.

"The Keeper of Gurnet Light [presumably Hannah Thomas] was unable to go to their aid because the harbor was blocked with ice. A causeway had to be built over the ice to rescue the survivors."

Nothing more is known about this first woman lighthouse keeper in the American colonies. The lights may have been extinguished during at least part of the war. John Thomas apparently did not survive the war; no records exist to indicate whether Hannah had children or what happened to her.[2] Many lighthouses after the war were put in the hands of veterans—mature and capable men who were eager to find good jobs—one of whom probably replaced her.

In 1790 the new federal government took over the 12 lighthouses on the Atlantic Coast, including Gurnet Point and five others in Massachusetts. The ninth law passed by the new Congress in 1789 created the lighthouse establishment—one of the earliest public works in the new republic—and placed it under the authority of an auditor in the Treasury Department. Every contract, large or small, as well as the appointment and salary of every keeper was personally approved by President Washington.

The lighthouse that Hannah Thomas tended during the Revolution was consumed by fire in 1801. When it was replaced in 1803, the Thomas family was paid $120 for the land on which the new light was built. Nothing remains of the first light save the eroded earthworks of the long-abandoned fort, which are still visible near the third lighthouse, rebuilt at the same location in 1842. Although the need for twin towers was eventually eliminated by more efficient aids to navigation, twin lights were maintained at Gurnet Point long after most others were abandoned—until in 1924 one of them was discontinued and the tower removed.

A single tower stood at Gurnet Point in 1958, surrounded by traces of Revolutionary War earthworks. Courtesy of the U.S. Coast Guard.

Hannah Thomas

1. NEW LAMPS TO LIGHT THE ATLANTIC COAST

As the new United States was coming into being, the flat-wick lamp was replaced in lighthouses by the spider lamp----a pan of oil with four or more wicks protruding from it. It had no chimney, and the acrid fumes given off by the spider lamp burned the eyes and nose, often driving the keeper out of the lantern housing. The intensity of the light depended on the lantern glass being kept clean and the wicks properly trimmed, and keepers became known as "wickies."

Who tended the 24 lighthouses on the East Coast in the first two decades of the 19th century is unknown. Official registers of keepers were not begun until 1828.

In 1812 the Argand lamp was introduced from England. This was a fountain lamp, consisting of an oil reservoir, a burner with a hollow circular wick and lamp chimney, and a parabolic reflector. The new lamp was smokeless. Because

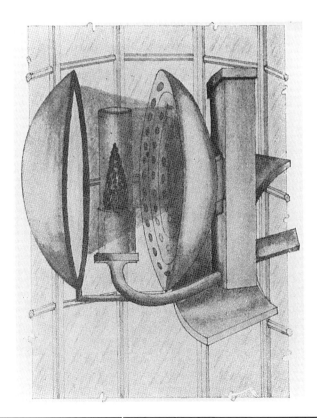

oxygen passed both inside and outside the wick, the flame burned much more brightly----equivalent to the light of seven candles (candlepower). A reflector behind the lamp further increased its brightness. A lighthouse might use from one to thirty of these lamps to provide adequate light.

Early American Argand type lamp with reflector and bull's eyes lens. Drawing taken from U.S. Coast Guard Aids to Navigation 1945.

Black Rock Light off Bridgeport, Connecticut, around 1880. Kate Moore assisted her father there from 1817 until 1871, then acted as official keeper from 1871 until 1879. The 1823 tower still stands. Courtesy of the National Archives, #26-LG-11-3.

Catherine Moore

III. Catherine Moore at Black Rock Light, Connecticut, 1817-1879

Catherine (Kate) Moore did not become official keeper of the Black Rock Light on the north shore of Long Island Sound until 1871 when she was 76 years old. Her father, Stephen Tomlinson Moore sought the keeper's post decades earlier, in 1817, after injuries from a fall aboard ship kept him from going to sea on the vessel in which he had invested. In 1889 Kate told a reporter from the *New York Sunday World*, "I was just 12 years old when I first began to assist my father in trimming the wicks. A few years after that his health began to fail and from then on I was practically the keeper."[3] She did her invalid father's work and cared for him for 54 years.

Kate's is the first voice to come directly to us from the ranks of women who kept the lights. "It was a miserable [light] to keep oing, nothing like those in use nowadays," she said of the fixed white light, which was 350 candlepower. "It consisted of eight oil lamps which took four gallons of oil each night, and if they were not replenished at stated intervals all through the night, they went out. During very windy nights it was almost impossible to keep them burning at all, and I had to stay there all night."

The light was located on Fayerweather Island, originally 200 acres of forest, but now shrunk by erosion to three scraggly acres of tall grasses and ailanthus trees (planted by Kate), stretching like a snake from Seaside Park in Bridgeport, Connecticut. "On [calm] nights I slept at home, dressed in a suit of boy's clothes, my lighted lantern hanging at my headboard and my face turned so that I could see shining on the wall the light from the tower and know if anything had happened."

If the light went out, Kate got up to tend to it. "Our house was forty rods from the lighthouse, and to reach it I had to walk across two planks under which on stormy nights were four feet of water. And it was not too easy to stay on those slippery, wet boards with the wind whirling and the spray blinding me."

Storms and gales were part of her life. "The island has been ruined by gales a number of times. Every fifty years these great gales come, the waves dashing clear over the island, and on Jan.

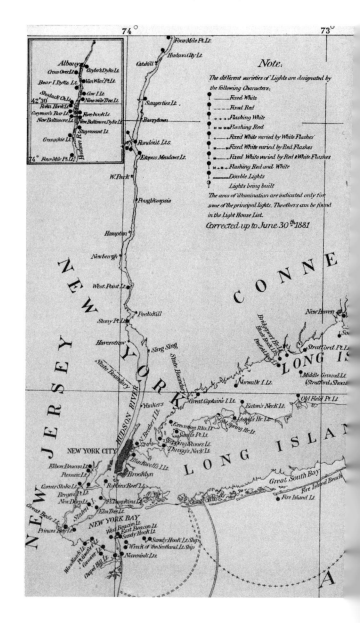

Catherine Moore

19, 1820, the last of the old trees [on Fayerweather Island] was swept away. The lighthouse itself blew over once when I was there (September 22, 1821). It was a dreadful thing to have happen, for this was then the only light on the Connecticut side of Long Island—the only light between New Haven and Eaton Neck—and was of course of inestimable value to mariners.

1881 Annual Report of the Lighthouse Board.

Sometimes there were more than 200 sailing vessels in here at night, and some nights there were as many as three or four wrecks, so you can judge how essential it was that they should see our light."

In the 72 years she was at Black Rock Light, Kate Moore saved at least 21 lives. "I wish it had been double that number. Of course there were a great many others, washed up on the shore, half-dead, whom we revived, and they all stayed with us until they received means to leave. They used to eat our provisions and the Government never paid us a cent for boarding them."

Kate Moore at age 94, ten years after her retirement as keeper of the Black Rock Light off Bridgeport, Connecticut. Courtesy of Historical Collections, Bridgeport Public Library.

Dead sailors washed up on the shore as well. "Hundreds!" Kate said. "We had to keep them, too, until the Government chose to dispose of them."

When asked whether she found the solitude of her life trying, Kate said that she had never known any other. "I never had much time to get lonely. I had a lot of poultry and two cows to care for, and each year raised twenty sheep, doing the shearing myself—and the killing when necessary. You see, in the winter you couldn't get to land on account of the ice being too thin, or the water too rough. Then in the summer I had my garden to make and keep. I raised all my own stuff, and as we had to depend on rain for our water, quite a bit of the time was consumed looking after that. We tried a number of times to dig for water, but always struck salt." These kinds of extracurricular activities were common for keepers in their efforts to make ends meet.

Kate did not consider her life unusually hard. "You see, I had done all this for so many years, and I knew no other life, so I was sort of fitted for it. I never had much of a childhood, as other children have it. That is, I never knew playmates. Mine were the chickens, ducks and lambs and my two Newfoundland dogs."

In spite of a complete lack of formal education, Kate Moore learned to read and collected a library of a hundred books— some given to her by visitors to the island. She also carried on such a thriving business planting, gathering, and seeding oyster beds in Long Island Sound that she owned the house to which she retired and left $75,000 in a bank account—a very substantial sum in those days—when she died in 1900.

Kate also carved duck decoys, selling them to visitors as souvenirs or to sportsmen who hunted. "I just took two blocks of wood and carved them out with a knife. It didn't take long to make one, and I liked to do it. I often worked at them in the nights when I had to stay up."

Kate Moore tended the Black Rock Light, the tower of which still stands, until she was 84 years old, retiring in 1878. Then she bought a retirement home, which still stands, and lived to age 105.

2. OTHER FEMALE LIGHTHOUSE KEEPERS IN THE EARLY 19TH CENTURY

Even before the federal register of lighthouse keeper appointments was begun in 1828, Mrs. Edward Shoemaker took up her dead husband's duties at Old Field Point Light on the north shore of Long Island. She served only two years—1826-27, but Walter Smith, who followed her, died very soon after. The appointment of his wife Elizabeth Smith to replace him in 1830 is recorded in the register of "Lighthouse Keepers and Assistants." She kept the light for the next 26 years.

She was succeeded by Mary Foster, who was perhaps her daughter, or at least related to her. A local newspaper, the *Long Island Star*, noted in 1869 that the Old Field Light had been in the care of the same family for over 40 years. Mary Foster was replaced that year, in spite of petitions signed by her friends, by a political appointee of the Grant administration.[4]

Also in 1830, Ann Davis succeeded her husband James as keeper of the Point Lookout Light at the entrance of the Potomac River in Maryland. He was the first keeper of that light, but died six months after his appointment. Ann's salary was $350, and her contract contained a notation forbidding the selling of liqueurs on the lighthouse premises. She served until 1847. Two other women kept the Point Lookout Light: Martha A. Edwards from 1852 to 1855, and her daughter Pamela Edwards from 1855 to 1869.[5]

Several other intrepid women kept lighthouses in the first half of the 19th century, some of them for a substantial number of years. Little information about them has survived, but their names should not be forgotten:

Barbara Mabrity's husband Michael, keeper of the Key West, Florida light, died of yellow fever in 1832, leaving her with six children. She took over his duties, and tended the 15 oil lamps until 1864 when she was 82. She survived four hurricanes, although in 1846 her children and eight others who had taken refuge in the tower drowned when the structure collapsed around them. Mrs. Mabrity's grandson William Bethel became keeper of the same light in 1889. When he retired in 1908, his wife Mary replaced him as keeper, remaining until 1914 with her son Merrill as her assistant.[6]

In 1834 Elizabeth Riley was appointed keeper of North Point Light in Maryland and stayed at her post until 1857.

Three women served as keepers of the Point Lookout Light on the Maryland side of the Potomac River. This 1883 view was taken by Major Jared A. Smith. Courtesy of the National Archives, #26-LG-24-5.

The first keeper at Morgan's Point Light, Connecticut, was a Captain Daboll, who won contracts to build several of the lighthouses on Long Island Sound. He kept the light from 1831 until 1838, when he died, leaving his wife Eliza with six small children. (Women in the 19th century generally averaged six or seven children each.) Mrs. Daboll's reputation was such that her letter of appointment from Washington said that she "belongs to that class of citizens whose standing in society is of the first responsibility." So conscientious was she, in fact, that when her light failed one night, she walked to the ferry in Groton to report the situation to the authorities in New London before word could reach them from any other source.[7] Mrs. Michaela Ingraham succeeded her husband Jeremiah at Pensacola Light, Florida, in 1840, remaining until 1855.

Patty Potter succeeded her husband at Stonington Light, Connecticut, in 1842. Unlike the many other women keepers who received glowing reports, the one remnant of information remaining about Patty Potter is negative. In October 1848 the Lighthouse Inspector reported that she "kept the most filthy house I have ever visited; everything appears to have been neglected." Lighthouse inspectors arrived unannounced. One can imagine a fastidious male catching a housewife/light keeper with dishes in the sink, children bickering, and beds unmade as she was tending to the lamps and the lantern. In any case, Patty remained at her post until 1854.[8]

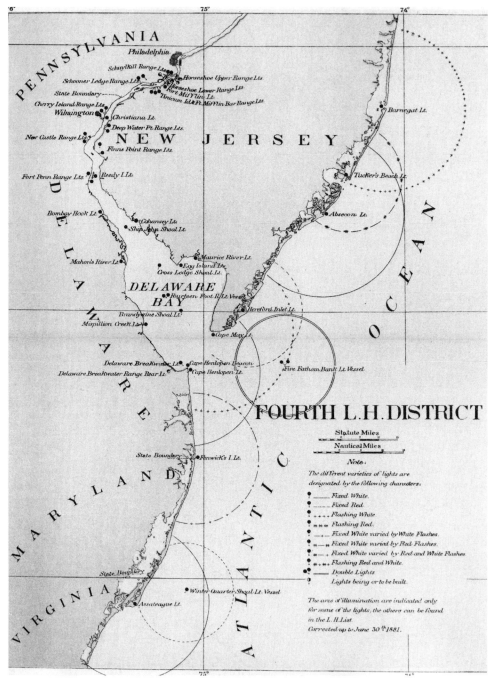

1881 Annual Report of the Lighthouse Board.

IV. Margaret Stuart at Bombay Hook Light, Delaware, 1850-1862

No words come directly from Margaret Stuart, who kept the Bombay Hook Light on the south side of the Smyrna River near the shore of the Delaware River from 1850 to 1862. The lighthouse—a white brick, two-story dwelling surmounted by a short tower and lantern room in the center of the roof—was built in 1831, rebuilt in 1841. Its first keeper was Duncan Stuart, Margaret's father. The lighthouse inspector reported in 1851 that Stuart (he spelled the name Stewart, but Margaret's official appointment in "Lighthouse Keepers and Assistants" lists her as Margaret Stuart) was 89 years old, and that his daughters did the actual work of keeping the station "neat and clean."

The inspector's report indicated that the Stuarts were tending Argand lamps under rather difficult conditions:

> Reflectors of thin copper and a very thin film of silver-plating, much worn off in spots; not firmly placed on the frame, and easily put out of adjustment. Lantern small, glass 8 x 12 inches; sashes thick and black—want painting very much; the frame of the dome and the lantern very dirty for want of paint, lantern leaks very much; until rebuilt, leaked in every part of building; tower so open it is difficult to carry a light into the lantern; wood-work rough and not planed; floor of lantern coppered; no curtains allowed; Captain Howard [presumably either the Lighthouse Engineer or Lampist] tinkered up the lamps and burners in May; four spare lamps, burners very common.

The inspector reported that Mr. Stewart had the lighthouse whitewashed at his own expense because there was no allowance for lime for whitewashing. The report made the dwelling sound rather primitive:

> House wants painting; spouts, etc., rusty for want of paint. Roof of the house very open—places a quarter of an inch between the shingles, brick-work rough; floors not tongued and grooved; rough and open in the attics;

garret rooms not plastered; wooden pillar, supporting steps, much worm-eaten; cellar in bad order—wants cementing and repairs; kitchen in cellar; oil smells baldly [sic].

In 1855 the *Annual Report of the Lighthouse Board* indicated that "new iron lanterns for fourth-order apparatus have been substituted for the old and defective style hitherto in use," and "superior French plate glass of very large dimensions" installed in the lantern. These should have made Margaret's duties a little less onerous.

Margaret Stuart's appointment ended, as did that of many other lighthouse keepers, during the Civil War. Many lights were extinguished then to prevent their aiding the enemy, and the confusion of the period affected the careers of many keepers.[9]

The Bombay Hook Lighthouse was abandoned some time before 1921. In 1974 it was either destroyed by fire or demolished as a hazard, with only the foundation remaining. The site is now the property of Delaware's Division of Fish and Wildlife and is part of the Bombay Hook Wildlife Refuge.

Bombay Hook Light in 1897. Courtesy of the National Archives, #26-LG-10-13B.

Margaret Stuart

3. A DANGEROUS OCCUPATION

Tales of tragedy were all too common in the lighthouse service. In 1718 the first keeper of the Boston Light, George Worthylake, was rowing his wife and daughter, along with a friend and a negro slave, between shore and the island in Boston Harbor where the light stood when their dory capsized in heavy seas. All were drowned----a foretaste of the many dangers to be faced by those who kept the lights. This incident made such an impression on a 13-year-old named Benjamin Franklin that he wrote a ballad----"The Lighthouse Tragedy"----which he printed and hawked on the streets of Boston, with great success.

Although women were generally not appointed to keep lighthouses in remote or dangerous locations, the nature of the work brought its own hazards. Cornelius Maher, keeper of the Oyster Beds Beacon on the north side of the Savannah River channel, drowned in 1853 while attempting to tow a brig to the city. His wife Mary kept the Beacon for the next three years. Charles Anderson, keeper of the Round Island Light in Pascagoula, Mississippi, drowned in 1872. His wife Margaret assumed his duties and continued as keeper until her death in 1881. Then her daughter Mary kept the lights burning for four months, until a new keeper was appointed.

Melissa Holden, wife of the keeper of the Deer Island Thoroughfare Light on Mark Island on the Penobscot Bay coast of Maine, delivered her youngest child in the 1870s with the help of her other four children when her husband was away on the mainland. On another occasion when her husband was away in Rockland, Melissa detected the sound of muffled oars as prowlers landed on the shore. When she heard the intruders under her bedroom window, she doused them with the contents of her chamber pot----successfully discouraging any further mischief.

Samuel Holden died in 1874, and Melissa applied for and was granted his appointment, but two years later was replaced by a male keeper. She then moved ashore, remarried, and had several more children, whose descendants still live in Stonington, Maine.[10]

Abbie Burgess, who assisted her father in keeping Matinicus Rock Light, in artist's rendering on the cover of Harper's Young People: An Illustrated Weekly, *May 2, 1882. Courtesy of Virginia State Library and Archives.*

V. Abbie Burgess at Matinicus Rock Light, Maine,1853-1872, and at White Head Light, Maine, 1875-1892

Abbie Burgess, who at age 14 moved with her family to the light station on Matinicus Rock off the coast of Maine, helped her father tend 28 Argand lamps. Her father won his appointment in 1853 and took with him his invalid wife and children—one son, Benji (who was generally away on fishing boats), and four daughters (of whom Abbie, born in 1839, was the eldest).

Matinicus Rock is a lonely, barren outcropping four miles off the south end of Matinicus Island. Twenty miles distant from the mainland, the original light station included two wooden towers for the lamps, attached to either end of the rectangular rubble-stone keeper's dwelling. Like most light stations, Matinicus Rock had small structures for a fog bell and other equipment, and perhaps even domestic animals. Sheds housed coal to provide heat, the oil used to fuel the lamps, and lifeboats. A cistern or rain shed collected fresh water.

The island's surface was a confused plain of loose stones and boulders, many of which moved when the waves swept over them at high tide. A boat slip with rails and winch was needed to launch a lifeboat and unload supplies. According to the *1891 Annual Report of the Lighthouse Board*, "There is a little cove where material can be hauled up in pleasant weather, but it has no harbor. The lighthouse keeper effects a landing by steering his boat through the breakers on top of a wave, so that it will land on the boatways, where his assistants stand ready to receive him and draw his boat so far up on the ways that a receding wave cannot carry it back to the sea."

The keeper's job revolved around maintaining the lamps, the twin towers[11] (built of stone in 1848), and the quarters. During the early 1800s, lighthouses used lamps that burned whale oil. A thick strain of whale oil was used in the summer, a thinner strain in the winter. In winter temperatures, even the thinner oil tended to congeal, forcing the keeper either to carry heated oil to the lantern or to keep a fire burning in a warming stove in the lantern of the lighthouse. The quality of the light depended on how well the wick was trimmed. All the accumulated soot had to be polished off the dustpans (reflectors) every day so that they would reflect the maximum light. The reliability of the lights was of great concern to keepers and mariners alike, for ships navigating perilous coasts in the 18th and 19th century depended on the lights to warn them away from danger. Sailors in those days still relied on the sun, stars, and primitive compasses to find their way, combining their knowledge of the tides, wind direction, water surfaces, cloud formations, and bird behavior to predict weather. Barometers of the time were crude kettle-shaped affairs in which the water level spilled over as pressure increased.

Rocks and shoals were extreme hazards in heavy weather as sailing ships sought their ports. Any failure of a light for even a short time could lead to disaster. Abbie learned to light the 28 Argand lamps that warned ships away from the dangerous ledges of Penobscot Bay and took her turn tending the lights and the stove during the night, permitting her father to spend part of his time fishing for lobsters and sailing to Rockland to sell them.

In January 1856 supplies were running desperately low because the lighthouse tender, which brought supplies twice a year, had failed to make its regular September call. Keeper Burgess decided to make a trip ashore to fetch food for his family and medicine for his sick wife. His son was away fishing, so Abbie was left in charge of the light. Soon after Burgess left, a storm blew in out of the northeast, and he was unable to return for four weeks. Sheets of spray crashed over the island, followed by sleet and snow. As the violence of the gale increased, Abbie moved her mother and younger sisters into one of the two light towers. Finally, at high tide, the waves washed completely over the island, destroying the old keeper's quarters. The women watched the destruction from the tower.

Many of the men and women who kept the lights had awesome tales to tell of the isolation of a lighthouse (particularly on remote islands), of the tedious daily tasks that kept the keeper tied to the post, of the personal danger of keeping the light during storms, of perilous rescues of wrecked seamen. Abbie Burgess, in a letter to a friend, gave a detailed description of that terrifying and exhausting month:

> You have often expressed a desire to view the sea out upon the ocean when it was angry. Had you been here on the 19 January, I surmise you would have been satisfied. Father was away. Early in the day, as the tide rose, the sea made a complete breach over the rock, washing every movable thing away, and of the old dwelling not one stone was left upon another of the foundation.
>
> The new dwelling was flooded and the windows [shutters] had to be secured to prevent the violence of the spray from breaking them in. As the tide came, the sea rose higher and higher, till the only endurable places were the lighttowers. If they stood we were saved, otherwise our fate was only too certain.

Matinicus Rock Light Station on an island off the coast of Maine, where Abbie Burgess assisted her father from 1853 to 1860. One of the 1857 towers continues as an active aid to navigation and the island, an important seabird nesting site, serves as a research headquarters for Audubon biologists. Courtesy of the U.S. Coast Guard.

But for some reason, I know not why, I had no misgivings and went on with my work as usual. For four weeks, owing to rough weather, no landing could be effected on the Rock. During this time we were without assistance of any male member of our family. Though at times greatly exhausted by my labors, not once did the lights fail. Under God I was able to perform all my accustomed duties as well as my father's.

You know the hens were our only companions. Becoming convinced, as the gale increased, that unless they were brought into the house they would be lost, I said to mother: "I must try to save them." She advised me not to attempt it. The thought, however, of parting with them without an effort was not to be endured, so seizing a basket, I ran out a few yards after the rollers had passed and the sea fell off a little, with the water knee deep, to the coop, and rescued all but one. It was

FIRST L.H. DISTRICT

*1881 Annual Report of the
Lighthouse Board.*

the work of a moment, and I was back in the house with the door fastened, but none too quick, for at that instant my little sister, standing at a window, exclaimed, "Oh, look! look there! the worst sea is coming!"

That wave destroyed the old dwelling and swept the Rock. I cannot think you would enjoy remaining here any great length of time for the sea is never still and when agitated, it roars, shuts out every other sound, even drowning our voices.

After the storm subsided, Abbie's father returned to find his family and the lights safe. A year later, under similar conditions, he was away from the rock for three weeks, but Abbie kept the lights burning. This time the family ran out of food supplies, and were down to one egg and one cup of corn meal a day when Burgess returned.

In 1857 new cylindrical granite towers, 48 feet tall, topped by lanterns in which third-order Fresnel lenses were installed, were constructed on Matinicus Rock (one of which is still lit today). The height of a tower depended on a calculation of the distance at which the light must be visible. Those towers in exposed locations were designed to withstand wind, waves, current, and ice, and the stability of the tower needed to be carefully computed to make it safe under the most severe conditions.

The price of whale oil quadrupled about this time, prompting a search for an alternate fuel. When it was discovered that lard oil worked well when burned at a high temperatures, the larger lamps were gradually switched from whale oil to lard oil.

Although Abbie's father lost his position to a new Republican appointee in 1860, Abbie stayed on to operate the beacon for the new keeper, then fell in love with his son. After she married Isaac H. Grant, Abbie acted as his assistant when he became keeper—one of over 250 women listed in "Lighthouse Keepers and Assistants" who held that post between 1828 and 1905. She received $440 a year for her services.

In 1869 a steam fog signal was established on Matinicus Rock, one of the first on the coast of Maine. Abbie had four children there, one of whom died and is buried there. She and her husband remained on Matinicus Rock until 1872 when they were transferred to White Head Light, near Spruce Head, Maine. There Abbie's salary as assistant keeper was increased to $480 annually. Abbie Burgess Grant's promotion to keeper at White Head Light is recorded in 1875 in "Lighthouse Keepers and Assistants." She and her husband served together as keepers at White Head until 1890, when her failing health led both of them to resign. She died two years later, having spent 37 of her 52 years in lighthouses.

Shortly before her death, she wrote her last letter:

> Sometimes I think the time is not far distant when I shall climb these lighthouse stairs no more. It has always seemed to me that the light was part of myself . . . . Many nights I have watched the lights my part of the night, and then could not sleep the rest of the night, thinking nervously what might happen should the light fail.

In all these years I always put the lamps in order in the morning and I lit them at night. These old lamps on Matinicus Rock . . . I often dream of them. When I dream of them it always seems to me that I have been away a long while, and I am hurrying toward the Rock to light the lamps there before sunset . . . . I feel a great deal more worried in my dreams than when I am awake.

I wonder if the care of the lighthouse will follow my soul after it has left this worn out body! If I ever have a gravestone, I would like it in the form of a lighthouse or beacon[12].

In 1945, many years after Abbie's death, lighthouse historian Edward Rowe Snow placed a miniature lighthouse on Abbie Burgess Grant's grave in Spruce Head Cemetery. Snow had for many years in the 1920s and 1930s flown his own plane to drop Christmas gifts by parachute to the lighthouse crews at offshore installations along the Maine coast. Abbie's story had obviously touched him.

White Head Light Station on Penobscot Bay in Maine, where Abbie Burgess Grant was official keeper from 1875 to 1892. The 1852 tower continues as an active aid to navigation. Courtesy of the National Archives, #26-LG-4-37.

4. ADOPTION OF THE FRESNEL LENS

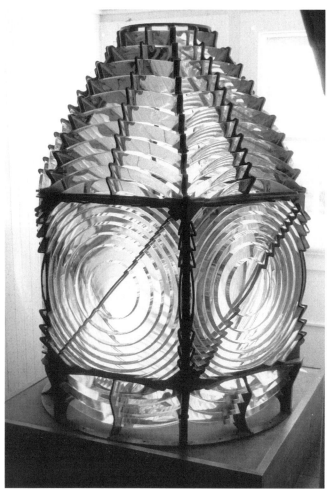

Fresnel lens on display at Hooper Strait Light, Chesapeake Bay Maritime Museum, St. Michaels, Maryland. Invented in France in 1822, Fresnel lenses are classified by "order," the first order being the largest (approximately 7 feet 10 inches in height, 72 7/16 inches in diameter) and the sixth order (1 foot 5 inches in height, 11 3/4 inches in diameter) the smallest. National Park Service photo by Candace Clifford.

In 1822 a new and very superior lens was developed in France. Fresnel's circular glass lens surrounded the lamp, with prisms at the top and bottom to reflect the light. The narrow sheet of refracted light was intensified by a powerful magnifying glass around the middle of the lens, resulting in a highly concentrated beam of light. The lens was accompanied by a so-called mechanical lamp, which burned oil pumped up from a reservoir below the level of the burner by means of weighted clockworks. Only one lamp was needed, with from one to four concentric wicks. The Fresnel lens came in seven sizes, the largest giving off the powerful light needed on an open seacoast. The smaller lenses were suitable for harbors.

The first Fresnel lenses in America were installed in the twin towers of Navesink Light Station on the New Jersey coast in 1840. A subsequent investigation by a board of specialists led Congress to order the use of Fresnel lenses in all new lighthouses, as well as in any others where earlier lamps were found inadequate.

5. CREATION OF THE LIGHTHOUSE BOARD

As maritime commerce increased and expanded into the Great Lakes, the Gulf of Mexico, and along the West Coast, many new lighthouses were built. Needless to say, administrative supervision by one man in the Treasury Department was no longer adequate to guarantee the efficient operation of so many aids to navigation. After a thorough investigation, Congress in 1852 created a nine-member Lighthouse Board to oversee the lighthouse service. Seven of its members were to be from the army or navy. The country was divided into 12 districts, with an inspector----a naval officer----and later a district engineer for each. The local customs collector----a political appointee----was still the supervisor in the field.

The Lighthouse Board systematically worked for the improvement of aids to navigation, including the preparation of correct charts giving accurate locations and descriptions of lighthouses so that they might more easily be recognized, both as landmarks by day and as beacons at night. Attention was given to color characteristics of the lights and distinctive patterns of flashing. The strength of each light's illumination was measured. An annual *Light List* was published, describing all aids to navigation in the United States and detailing the distinctive characteristics of all lights and lighthouses.[13]

Biloxi Light on the Gulf of Mexico, kept by Mary Reynolds from 1854 to 1866, by Maria Younghans from 1867 to 1919, and by Miranda Younghans from 1919 to 1929. Courtesy of the National Archives, #26-LG-34-22A.

VI. Mary Reynolds, 1854-1866, Maria Younghans, 1867-1919, and Miranda Younghans, 1919-1929, at Biloxi Light, Mississippi

Women tended the light at Biloxi, Mississippi—the most prominent landmark on the Mississippi Gulf Coast—for more years than any other light in the United States. Mary Reynolds was in charge from 1854 to 1866. She was followed by Mrs. Maria Younghans, keeper from 1867 to 1918. Maria's daughter Miranda followed her and held her post until 1929. Although these three women racked up three-quarters of a century of continuous and dedicated service, almost no personal information about them survived their retirement, in part because they left no descendants to treasure their memories.

Built in 1847, the Biloxi tower was prefabricated of cast iron (possibly the first in the South to be so constructed), with a balustrade encircling the watch room, and was brought by ship to its permanent location along the roadbed of the Old Spanish Trail. Today the tower rests on a circular concrete base in the median of a major highway, U.S. 90, and is surrounded by a circular iron fence.

A sea wall was constructed in 1854 to protect the site from the tides and storms, and periodic repairs were required to keep erosion from tilting the tower. While the light itself stood 53 feet above the ground, its elevation put it 61 feet above sea level. The original illuminating apparatus consisted of nine cast brass lamps with separate reflectors. Its three-second flashing light marked the entrance to Biloxi Harbor for the many schooners which once plied the Mississippi Sound and Gulf waters in search of shrimp and oysters. It welcomed, too, those schooners which sought a lumber cargo on the Tchouticabouffa River and other inland waterways.

Mrs. Mary Reynolds sought the aid of Mississippi's newly elected senator, Albert Gallatin Brown, to obtain her appointment in 1854 as second keeper of the Biloxi Light. Her annual salary was $400. When the Civil War broke out, the patriots of Biloxi wanted the light extinguished so that it could not aid Yankee ships, and Mrs. Reynolds worried about her responsibility for the federal stores in her possession.

She turned to the governor for assistance in influencing the local men. Her letter is in the Mississippi Department of Archives and History.[14]

Biloxi, Nov. 26th, 1861

To His Excellency Gov. Pettus
Dear Sir,

With the request that you will pardon my informality in my letter, I beg to inform you that I am a woman entirely unprotected. I have for several years past been the Keeper of the Light House at Biloxi, the small salary accruing from which has helped me to support a large family of orphaned children.

These children being heirs at law to considerable property in Maryland, I have yearly received a stipend through the Hon. Henry May of Baltimore who is the Executor of their estates. Owing to our political rupture [the Civil War started in April 1861] I cannot hope for any immediate assistance from Mr. May.

I do not know if my [federal] salary as the Keeper of the Light House will be continued.

On the 18th of June last, the citizens of Biloxi ordered the light to be extinguished which was immediately done and shortly after others came and demanded the key of the Light Tower which has ever since remained in the hands of a Company calling themselves "Home Guards."

At the time they took possession of the Tower it contained valuable Oil, the quantity being marked on my books. I have on several occasions seen disreputable characters taking out the oil in bottles. Today they carried away a large stone jug capable of containing several gallons. They may take also in the night as no one here appeared to have any authority over them.

Their Captain, J. Fewell, is also Mayor of the City of Biloxi, and if you would have the kindness to write him orders to have the oil measured and placed under my charge at the dwelling of the Light House I would be very grateful to you for so doing.

I write to you merely as a Light Keeper believing that injustice has been and is still doing here. I can give you unquestionable reference as regards to my character.

I am a native of Baltimore and for many years a citizen of Mobile. Sad reverses of fortune and the care of so many orphan children of my deceased relatives rendered it necessary that I should exert myself to the uttermost for their support.

I have ever faithfully performed the duties of Light Keeper in storm and sunshine attending it. I ascended the Tower at and after the last destructive storm (1860) when men stood appalled at the danger I encountered.

After the Light was extinguished, I wrote to New Orleans and offered my services to make Volunteer Clothing [for Confederate soldiers]. Received a large bale of heavy winter clothing which I made during the hottest season of the year working day and night to have them done in time.

I do not speak thus of myself through vanity or idle boasting but to assure you that I have tried to do my share in our great and holy cause of freedom.[15]

The governor's reply is not available, and Mrs. Reynolds was listed as official keeper until 1866—although the light may have remained dark until that year. (Some lights during the Civil War had women keepers paid by the Confederate government.)

Perry Younghans succeeded Mary Reynolds as keeper of the Biloxi Light. Owner of a nearby brick yard which had been shelled and destroyed by northern forces, he used political influence to obtain his appointment after the war. He died within the year. His wife Maria assumed her husband's duties and continued at her post until 1919, winning the highest approval from the inspectors for her services. The bare bones of Maria's tenure can be gleaned from the annual reports of the Lighthouse Board. In 1866 the illuminating apparatus was changed to a fixed Fresnel lens of the 5th order, with Franklin lamps which burned lard oil. The light was visible 13 miles in clear weather.

In 1876 the damaged brick wall was replaced by a heavy timber bulkhead. In 1877 the keeper's house was described as "so far decayed as to render it difficult to make any repairs." In 1880 the house was torn down and a new one built. In 1888 "a new fence was put up all around the premises, the wash-house and wood-shed were rebuilt, and various other repairs made." A storm that same year did such damage to the breakwater that it had to be rebuilt again.

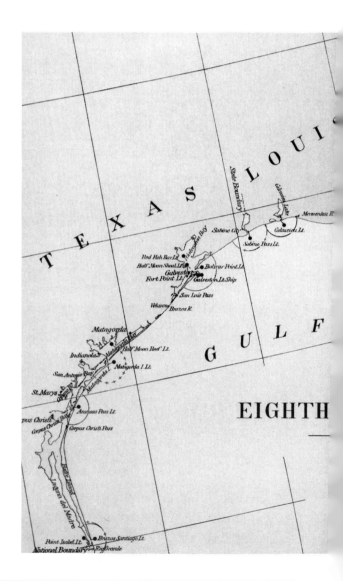

Mary Reynolds, Maria Younghans, and Miranda Younghans

An appointment as extended as Maria Younghans's should have left behind interesting memorabilia, but a few newspaper clippings provide the extent of what we know of her half-century-long career. In the Biloxi and Gulfport *Daily Herald* of August 22, 1925, an obituary states that Maria Younghans "in the winter of 1870 called her brother-in-law, and effected through him the rescue of a man being swept out to sea about daylight, clinging to an upturned boat; and during the 1916 storm, when the heavy glass in the lighthouse tower was

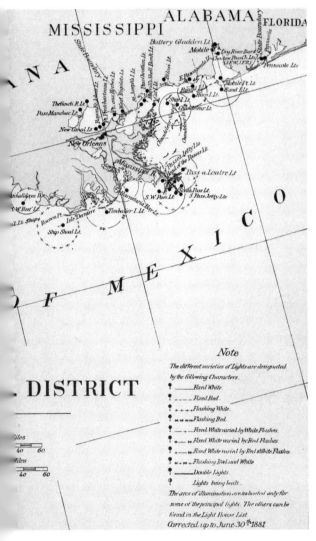

1881 Annual Report of the Lighthouse Board.

Miranda Younghans, who kept the Biloxi Light from 1919 until 1929. Courtesy of Biloxi Public Library.

broken by a large pelican being blown against it, she and her daughter, mindful of the especial need of the light on such a night, replaced the glass temporarily and made the 'light to shine' as before, unimpaired." An 1893 edition of the New Orleans *Daily Picayune*, reporting on a hurricane, stated that "Mrs. (Maria) Younghans, the plucky woman who was in charge of the Biloxi light, kept a light going all through the storm, notwithstanding that there were several feet of water in the room where she lived." The Lighthouse Board reported that the storm again destroyed the breakwater, but repairs were not completed until 1895.

Subsequent Lighthouse Board annual reports mention construction of brick walks, stable, washhouse, picket fence, and chicken house. The size of the oil house was doubled, and "a 900-foot wharf with a gate landing platform, steps, and boat davits at the outer end was built." A boathouse on piles was added later at the outer end of the wharf. In 1906 the old cisterns were removed and municipal waterworks installed.

As Maria aged, her daughter Miranda acted as her assistant, taking over many of her duties, and assuming all of them when Maria retired. The light was electrified in 1926, during Miranda's tenure. She retired in 1929.

The Biloxi and Gulfport *Daily Herald* carried Miranda's obituary on February 6, 1933, noting "her unfailing courtesy and dignity gave hundreds of casual visitors to the light house a beautiful memory of her, and a visit to the light house was always described with many references to Miss Younghans."

In mid-20th century the Biloxi Light was automated and the tower deeded to the city which maintains the light as a private aid to navigation. The keeper's quarters was destroyed by hurricane Camille in 1969.[16]

Biloxi Lighthouse currently sits on the median strip of U.S. Highway 90. Courtesy of the U.S. Coast Guard.

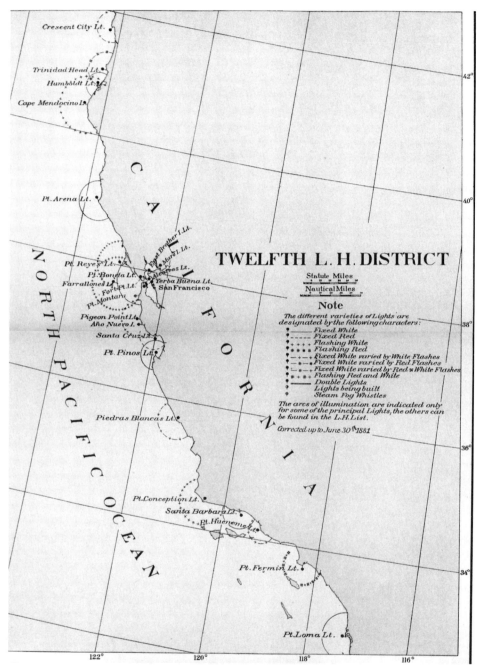

Crescent City Lt.

Trinidad Head Lt.
Humboldt Lt.

Cape Mendocino I.

C A L I F O R N I A

Pt. Arena Lt.

N O R T H   P A C I F I C   O C E A N

East Brother I. Lt.
Mare I. Lt.
Pt. Reyes Lt.
Alcatraz Lt.
Pt. Bonita Lt.
Yerba Buena Lt.
Farrallones Lt.
Fort Pt. Lt.
San Francisco
Pt. Montara

Pigeon Point Lt.
Año Nuevo I.
Santa Cruz Lt.

Pt. Pinos Lt.

Piedras Blancas Lt.

Pt. Conception Lt.
Santa Barbara Lt.
Pt. Hueneme Lt.

Pt. Fermin Lt.

Pt. Loma Lt.

TWELFTH L. H. DISTRICT

Statute Miles

Nautical Miles

Note

The different varieties of Lights are
designated by the following characters:

Fixed White
Fixed Red
Flashing White
Flashing Red
Fixed White varied by White Flashes
Fixed White varied by Red Flashes
Fixed White varied by Red & White Flashes
Flashing Red and White
Double Lights
Lights being built
Steam Fog Whistles

The arcs of illumination are indicated only
for some of the principal Lights, the others can
be found in the L.H. List.

Corrected up to June 30th 1881

42°

40°

38°

36°

34°

122°   120°   118°   116°

1881 Annual Report of the Lighthouse Board.

Lights on the West Coast

6. ADOPTION OF ECLIPSERS

Navigators were learning, as the various lighthouses were being built on the East Coast, that techniques for distinguishing one light from another were essential. The number of visible lights, their color and intensity were important, but the most effective method by far was the use of flashing lights. The first "eclipsers" were installed in the Cape Cod Light in 1797. In 1817 a revolving mechanism was installed in Sandy Hook Light, "with eighteen lamps and reflectors, on a triangular frame, performing a revolution every five minutes; the utmost power of light will appear three times each revolution." Experiments in developing mechanisms to speed the revolution of a lens continued throughout the 19th century, resulting eventually in lights that flashed in a matter of seconds.

7. LIGHTS ON THE WEST COAST

Because ships were still the prevalent form of transportation in the first half of the 19th century, California's maritime heritage is linked to the opening up of the Pacific Coast. California's shoreline is, in many ways, very inhospitable. For the early settlers the most noticeable difference between the East Coast and the West Coast was the lack of natural harbors. The Pacific was plagued with fierce winter storms, but in the 1,810 miles between the Mexican and Canadian borders, only San Diego, San Francisco, and the Strait of Juan de Fuca provided natural harbors sufficient to ride out very rough weather. The rocky, irregular coastline abounded with unmarked dangers----reefs, ledges, offshore rocks, islands, and spectacularly tall points of land jutting far out into the ocean. Navigation in many areas was hampered by frequent days of heavy fog, making fog signals almost as important as shore beacons.

7. LIGHTS ON THE WEST COAST cont.

Not until 1840, during the war with Mexico, did United States forces occupy California, and in 1848 the Treaty of Guadalupe Hidalgo ceded California to the United States. A naval base was immediately established in San Francisco Bay. The discovery of gold that same year led thousands of people to pour into the mines of the Sierra Nevada. The sea routes drew the heavy traffic in the first months of the Gold Rush, promoting competition to turn out the fastest and fleetest clipper ships to make the trip around the Horn. After 1850 a thriving coastal trade in lumber increased maritime commerce.

The completion of the transcontinental railroad in 1869 ended California's isolation, but sailing ships were still the cheapest way to move bulk cargoes----competing as best they could with the rapidly developing steamship, which soon made possible trade across the Pacific. All these ships needed aids to navigation to guide them along the treacherous Pacific Coast.

A large number of light stations, including substantial towers designed to hold Fresnel lenses, were constructed on the California coast between 1854 and 1910. The first lighthouses, built in the 1850s, were designed in Washington, and were typically Cape Cod structures with a tower rising through the center of the keeper's quarters. Little thought was given at first to the particularities of California's landscapes. Because wood was plentiful and cheap, they were built of redwood.[17]

VII. Charlotte Layton, 1856-1860, and Emily Fish, 1893-1914, at Point Pinos Light, California; Juliet Nichols at Angel Island Light, California, 1902-1914

In 1855 Charles Layton, native of Oxfordshire, England, and veteran ordnance sergeant of a U.S. Army artillery regiment, became first keeper of Point Pinos Light Station at the entrance to Monterey Bay—the oldest continuously operating lighthouse on the West Coast. He brought his wife Charlotte (a native of Beaufort, North Carolina), three sons, and one daughter to the drab Cape Cod bungalow with the light tower in the center of its roof. That same year Layton was killed while serving as a member of a sheriff's posse chasing a notorious outlaw, causing the local collector of customs (who oversaw lighthouses) to write the Lighthouse Board in Washington, D.C., as follows: "By this dispensation of providence, his widow, Charlotte A. Layton and four children have been left entirely destitute. I authorized her to continue at the post occupied by her late husband, and she is now discharging all the duties of principal keeper of the Lights at Point Pinos. I take much pleasure in recommending her for the place of principal keeper: she is a person eminently qualified for the position: she is industrious and bears an unblemished reputation."

Enclosed was a petition signed by a group of citizens in Monterey. "You will have the goodness," the collector of customs wrote, "to present the memorial to the Hon. Secretary of the Treasury and urge the confirmation of the appointment." The appointment followed promptly in 1856.

The lamp Charlotte tended burned whale oil, forced up from a tank by a gravity-operated piston. Its beam was concentrated by a third-order Fresnel lens manufactured in France. A falling-weight mechanism rotated a metal shutter around the light, causing the beam to be cut off to seaward 10 out of every 30 seconds. The weights were wound by hand. Title to the land on which the lighthouse stood was in dispute during Charlotte's entire tenure, and not settled until 1880.

Charlotte Layton was paid $1,000 a year, a salary much higher than that prevailing on the East Coast because the supply of available labor in California lagged behind demand. Men outnumbered women twelve to one, but the men were largely attracted to the gold fields, giving women a wider range of employment opportunities. Charlotte had a male assistant keeper who earned $800. In 1860 Charlotte married her assistant, George Harris. Although the lighthouse service permitted a man to be in a subordinate role to a woman, Charlotte stepped down to again become assistant keeper. (In similar circumstances, Laura Blach, who was appointed keeper of the Ediz Hook Light at Port Angeles, Washington, in 1874, married the local customs collector. She, however, kept her keeper's position, with Thomas Stratton becoming her assistant.)

After their retirement, the Harrises leased and ran the old Washington Hotel in Monterey. George Harris was listed in the 1870 census as a hotelkeeper. Charlotte died in 1896.

Three decades after Charlotte Layton's tenure, the ambiance of Point Pinos Light Station was drastically changed. In 1893 widowed Emily Fish introduced to the modest Cape Cod bungalow a Chinese servant and furnishings seldom seen in a lighthouse—antique furniture, good paintings, fine china and old silver, leather-bound books. The servant Que had come with Emily from China when her husband gave up his consular post there. The furnishings came from the elegant house in Oakland where she and Dr. Melancthon Fish had lived after he established a private medical practice and began teaching at the University of California.

Emily was 50 when her husband died. Her naval officer son-in-law, who was Inspector of the 12th district of the lighthouse service, mentioned casually one day that the keeper of the Point Pinos Light Station was about to retire. Emily decided she would like the post, and her son-in-law arranged her appointment.

Point Pinos Light Station included 92 acres of sand and scrub. After transforming the keeper's house, Emily had topsoil brought in and spread so she and Que could plant trees, grass, and a cypress hedge around the yard. Then she added Thoroughbred horses to pull her carriage. Holstein cows grazed around the station, white leghorn chickens provided eggs, French poodles greeted visitors. As her mourning period ended, Emily rejoined the social life of the Monterey Peninsula, giving small dinner parties for artists and writers, and naval officers from ships calling in Monterey Bay.

Authorized to employ laborers to help with the heavy work around the station, Emily listed in her log more than 30 male workers during her years as keeper—and stated that most of them were discharged for incompetence. Inspectors invariably noted that the Point Pinos Light Station was in excellent condition. In 1902 a tract of 52 acres lying between the light

1859 drawing of the Point Pinos Light Station in Pacific Grove, California, after an 1855 sketch by Major Hartman Bache. Courtesy of the National Archives, #26-LG-66-64.

1874 MONTH.	DAY.	RECORD OF IMPORTANT EVENTS AT THE STATION, BAD WEATHER, &c.
April	1	Wind Light — W. Clear —
	2	" " W.
	3	" " N.W. "
	4	" " W. Hazy —
	5	" " W. Hazy —
	6	" " N.W. Hazy — partly clear —
	7	" Fresh W. to S. Hazy. Foggy morning —
	8	" Light W. Clear —
	9	" S.W. Clear —
	10	" Fresh W. to S. Hazy — Foggy morning
	11	" S.W. Clear — Steamer bd. south.
	12	" Light W. " " bd. out south.
	13	" Light W.
	14	" Fresh N.W. Clear
	15	" Strong N.W. Clear — Partly cloudy
	16	" N.W. Clear —
	17	" Light N.N. to S. Hazy — Foggy night
	18	" " N.W. — "
	19	" " S.W. — "
	20	" " S.W. " Foggy —
	21	" Fresh S. Cloudy — Shower —.05
	22	" " S.W. Cloudy — Steamer pass'd South — 9 P.M. the night of the 21st on a sunken rock the Eureka going on her trip South of to wind.
	23	" Light S.W. Clear — Steamer pass'd South
	24	" " S.W. Cloudy — Fresh at night
	25	" Variable S.B. Rain, & Hail, .12 —
	26	" Fresh S.E. Rain in showers .35
	27	" Fresh W. — Rain showery — .28
	28	" Fresh N.W. Cloudy — clearing —
	29	" " Variable N.W. to S.E. Cloudy — Fog at night
	30	" Light variable N.W. to S.E. Hazy —

Charlotte Layton, Emily Fish, and Juliet Nichols

Emily A. Fish Keeper—

Steamer bd in & out South
Lumber schooner bd in.
Steamer bd in & out South. Steamer from the north & out.
Steamer bd in & out South. Laborer D.Y.S. Brewer came on duty to day.
Lumber schooner bd out.

No vessels seen.

Keeper left the station at 6 A.M. on three days leave, having provided substitute.
2 steamers passed north.
Returned to station at 6.30 P.M. everything in order —
Steamer bd in & out South.
Steamer passed north.

Steamer passed.

Steamer bd in & out South
Very thick, no fog.
Steamer Eureka brought the survivors of the steamer Los Angeles which was wrecked at
two miles below Point Sur to north. Survivors & crew were sent by rail to San Francisco.
Sailing vessel passed north.
Five bodies were brought to Monterey from Point Sur. Coroner inquest
broken verdict of manslaughter against 1st mate Ryf Kregel —
Steamer bd from north & out. Trucking schooner in tow of tug Fearless bd in,
Steamer bd in from the South. Trucking scow San Pedro in tow tug Fearless—put back.
in port unable to face the weather. 27 2 Steamer passed South.
Tug Fearless bd out South & returned to port —
Steamer passed north.
Steamer bd in & out South

Pages from the official log for the month of April 1894, kept by Emily Fish at Point Pinos Light. Courtesy of the National Archives.

station and the sea was purchased so that stores and supplies could be landed from tenders.[18]

The inspector who had arranged Emily Fish's appointment had married her niece and stepdaughter Juliet, daughter of her sister, who was Dr. Fish's first wife and had died in childbirth in China. Emily had raised Juliet as her own child and seen her married, at age 30, to Lt. Commander Henry E. Nichols. Commander Nichols, after his service as Lighthouse Inspector, was sent to the Philippines and died in 1898 during the Spanish-American War. As the wife of a former lighthouse service officer, Juliet was offered the post at the Angel Island Light in San Francisco Bay in 1902. She tended a fogbell and an uncovered fifth-order lens with a fixed red light, which was moved by pulley out of the bell house each evening.

Emily Fish and Juliet Nichols were both on duty at their respective lighthouses early on the morning of April 18, 1906, to experience firsthand one of the world's most severe earthquakes. Emily was making her final rounds around 5 a.m. when she became aware of odd noises coming from the barn—the horses pounding the barn floor and the cows lowing uneasily. She went to the watch room to scan the landscape through the windows, seeking whatever was disturbing the animals.

Emily wrote in her log that the first tremor of the "violent and continued earthquake" jarred the lighthouse at 5:13 a.m. The building shook and swayed, while cracking noises and tinkling sounds of breaking glass came from the tower. Outside the window trees whipped and swayed.

The noises, the shaking of the earth, and the trembling of the building lasted for about two minutes. Emily and Que rushed up the stairs of the tower, noting as they climbed that a crack in the brickwork and coping of the tower was much enlarged. In the lantern the shock had bent a connecting tube and jarred the damper so that the lamp flame had run up much higher than it should. The violent tremors continued as they fought to control the flame.

When the tremors finally ended, the two surveyed the whole station to assess the damage that had been done. The granite walls of the lighthouse had withstood the shocks, but the water in the woodhouse tank was thrown out on the floor. In the lantern, the prisms in the Fresnel lens had been jarred and

Emily A. Fish, who kept the Point Pinos Light in Pacific Grove, California, from 1893 to 1914. Courtesy of Monterey Public Library

had struck against each other, making the tinkling sound she had heard. When Emily attempted to report the damage to the district office in San Francisco, she found all telegraphic and telephone communication beyond Salinas, ten miles away, cut off. The train track was also obstructed, with no trains able to run.[19]

The *1906 Annual Report of the Lighthouse Board* reported that "the damage was so great that it became necessary to tear down and rebuild the tower with reinforced concrete." In 1907 the repairs were completed. "The lantern and lens were removed for about 5 feet below the lantern floor. The original walls were of brick masonry 1 foot thick. The tower was rebuilt of reenforced concrete of the same thickness and general design. The reenforcing metal, consisting of ¾-inch diameter rods laid vertically 8 inches apart, was set in holes drilled into the remaining walls; horizontal rings of ⅝-inch diameter wire cable were used to fasten the vertical rods. The station is supplied with water from the mains of the town of Pacific Grove. Minor repairs were made. A new 2-inch pipe, 2,200 feet long, was laid and connected with an elevated 4,000-gallon redwood tank. The tank is on the framed support and affords an efficient fire protection for the station."[20]

Juliet Nichols, at her post on Angel Island in San Francisco Bay on that fateful day in 1906, was making a final check of her equipment when she heard a rumbling sound. She looked across the water to the city silhouetted against the hills and was astonished to see buildings on the waterfront collapsing. Snatching her field glasses, she watched, horrified, as familiar landmarks crumbled into rapidly mounting piles of rubble. As the subterranean tremors continued, fires broke out, raging through factories, homes, and office buildings, until the skyline was blackened with smoke and ash.

Isolated on her island, Juliet watched the conflagration helplessly, trying to grasp the enormity of the tragedy unfolding before her eyes. Later she would learn that the earthquake had damaged every community within 100 miles of San Francisco.

Less than three months after that great disaster, Angel Island's fog signal broke down. According to the annual report of the Lighthouse Board, a new striking apparatus had been installed in 1905. Juliet was watching the fog roll in through the Golden Gate, as it so regularly does, and listening to the foghorns start up in lighthouses on both sides of the channel. She rushed to start her own equipment, only to have the machinery cough into silence a few minutes later. She could see the masts of a sailing vessel approaching above the fog. With no time for repairs, she snatched a hammer and began pounding the bell, warning the ship away from her island. In her report on the malfunctioning of the equipment, she wrote that she pounded the bell at the prescribed intervals for twenty hours before the fog finally lifted.

Mechanical fog signals were notorious for breaking down. The mechanical pounding of the fogbell produced strong vibrations, which caused tension bars and hammer springs to break, even snapping the rope attached to the clockwork weight. The chapter entitled "Instructions for the Use and Management of Fog Signals" in *Instructions to Light-Keepers*[21] is one of the longest and most complex sections in the manual issued to light keepers.

Two days later the Angel Island machinery failed again, forcing Juliet to repeat her exhausting ordeal. When the weather cleared, she summoned the lighthouse engineer to make

Charlotte Layton, Emily Fish, and Juliet Nichols

Fog bell ringing mechanism in Hooper Strait Lighthouse, Chesapeake Bay Maritime Museum, St. Michaels, Maryland. National Park Service photo by Candace Clifford.

repairs. Juliet Nichols's whole career at Angel Island was a battle with fog. Her log recorded periods of fog as long as 80 hours at a time, with repeated incidents when she struck the bell by hand.

Why not, if a fog signal fails, just throw up your hands? Ships continued coming and going, fog or no fog, and the lighthouse keeper's duty was to prevent their wrecking themselves on the hazards along the shipping lanes. Angel Island was one of the worst hazards in San Francisco Bay, and Juliet Nichols took her duties very seriously. She richly deserved the commendations she earned for her dedication.

In 1914 both women retired. Emily Fish bought a house in Pacific Grove, where she lived quietly until her death at age 88 in 1931. Juliet lived equally privately in the hills of Oakland until her death in 1947. In the Pleasant Hill Cemetery in Oakland, the Fish/Nichols plot has two headstones bearing the

In 1992, the 1855 Point Pinos Lighthouse continued as the oldest active aid to navigation on the West Coast. National Park Service photo by Candace Clifford.

names of Dr. M. W. Fish and Capt. Nichols, but nothing to indicate that two dedicated lighthouse keepers, Emily Fish and Juliet Nichols, lie there beside them.[22]

VIII. Catherine A. Murdock at Rondout Creek Light, New York, 1857-1907

The first lighthouse at the entrance of Rondout Creek on the west side of the Hudson River was constructed of wood in 1837. George W. Murdock took his wife and two small children to that station in 1856, and found that the structure was already damaged by weather and ice. Although it was rickety and its safety questioned, Catherine Murdock was too preoccupied with producing a third child to give much thought to her surroundings.

Within a year after his appointment, George Murdock, who had gone ashore to purchase groceries, was found drowned— lying in the water beside his loaded boat, apparently on his way back to the lighthouse. Despite the tragedy and the attention her young children required, Catherine Murdock continued faithfully to maintain the light.

Others applied for her late husband's position, but local friends cited her diligence in her duties and recommended Mrs. Murdock for the post, to which she was appointed in 1857. She spent a decade (including the Civil War years) in the old lighthouse, which was threatened repeatedly by severe storms and spring flooding. One storm in particular was so fierce that "the house rocked to and fro like a church steeple." Although Catherine feared the building might collapse, she knew how hazardous the river would be for boatmen without the light to keep them on course. She stayed at her post and kept the light shining in the tower.

In 1867 a new lighthouse (now known as Rondout I) was constructed of bluestone on the south side of the creek entrance. The lantern was inside a square granite tower in the northeast angle of the dwelling on a round granite pier. The keeper's house was a solid, cozy structure with four rooms on each of its two floors; a local newspaper described it as "a little waterborne castle." Photographs of the time show the family parlor filled with dark Victorian furniture and the walls hung with framed photographs and prints.

Catherine Murdock lived more than forty years in her castle. From her island home she witnessed the sinking of the passenger steamboat *Dean Richmond* and the burning of the steamboats *Thorn* and *Clifton* and the barge *Gilboa*. She told a newspaper reporter that the sight of the *Clifton* filled her with awe—one mighty mass of flame as it drifted in the current down the Hudson. She and her son rescued several seamen, nursing some back to health, but seldom reported these efforts because she disliked filling out the required paper work.

One morning, before dikes were built on each side of the Rondout Creek entrance, Catherine's peaceful sewing was interrupted by a loud crash and the splintering of glass. She turned around and found a schooner's bowsprit sticking through the window and halfway into her room. The schooner had been crowded into the lighthouse by a steam tug towing a line of barges out of Rondout Creek.

Catherine found the lighthouse very pleasant in summer, when 20 or 30 visitors a day stopped by to climb the tower. But winters were cold and dreary, punctuated by "heavy and perilous storms." The worst experience that Mrs. Murdock recalled was a flood in December of 1878. On the previous day, as a very heavy snowstorm turned into pouring rain, a family friend visiting the lighthouse urged Catherine to go safely ashore. She replied, "I'm a woman, I know, but if the Lighthouse goes down tonight, I go with it."

When she climbed the tower at midnight to replace the lamps, all she could hear in the pitch dark night was the roar of rushing, rising water. At 3 a.m., the dam at Eddyville upstream on Rondout Creek gave way. The flood carried away houses and barns, tore boats, barges, and tugs from their moorings, and swept everything down the raging current. Catherine could hear the crashing in the darkness, but the lighthouse stood firm, the light shining brightly in the tower. When daylight revealed her surroundings, the flats were strewn with wrecks, and a schooner rested on top of the dike, with a live horse trembling beside it. The horse plunged into the water and swam a mile to shore.

In 1880 Catherine's son James was appointed assistant keeper. He and his wife lived in the lighthouse with his mother. Mrs. Murdock, who had remarried in the interim, retired in

1907 and moved ashore. James succeeded her as official keeper, remaining until 1915 when Rondout I was replaced with a three-story Rondout II, set on a concrete pier.

Rondout I was dismantled in the 1950s. Rondout II light was automated in 1954, and the building leased in 1984 to the Hudson River Maritime Museum, which now uses it as an exhibit area.[23]

Catherine Murdock, keeper of Rondout Creek Lighthouse on the Hudson River from 1867 to 1907. These woodcut illustrations appeared in the Kingston Daily Freemen *around 1888. Courtesy of the Rondout Lighthouse Collection, Hudson River Maritime Museum, Kingston, New York.*

LIGHT-HOUSE ESTABLISHMENT.
Form 206.

JOURNAL of Light-Station at St. Marks Fla

MONTH	DAY	RECORD OF IMPORTANT EVENTS AT THE STATION, BAD WEATHER, ETC.
June	1	Light Southerly breeze
	2	Light E breeze to S & S E
	3	Moderate E breeze in the morning Hazy
	4	Calm in the morning Hazy dry
	5	Moderate Southerly breeze
	6	Fresh E breeze to S E
	7	Light E breeze in the morning Cloudy
	8	Light E breeze in the morning Cloudy
	9	Light E breeze in the morning Cloudy
	10	Light E breeze in the morning Cloudy Hazy
	11	Moderate E breeze to S & S E
	12	Moderate variable winds
	13	Fresh S & E breeze to S & S E
	14	Fresh S & E breeze to E
Inspection		Received Lt. Ho. Inspection
	15	Fresh S E breeze to S E
	16	Light variable winds S E
Inspection	17	received Lt. Ho. Inspection Sky
		Light S E breeze to S
	18	Moderat variable Winds
	19	Light S breeze to S W
	20	Light S breeze in the moring cloudy
	21	Fresh S breeze S S W
	23	Moderat S breeze to S W
	24	Light Southerly breeze
	25	Calm in the moring Hazy dry
	26	Light variable Winds S E
	27	Light S breeze to S W
	28	Moderat E breeze in moing
	29	Calm in the moring Hazy
	30	Fresh breeze to S E

Mrs Sarah J Fine
Keeper

8. KEEPERS' LOGS

All lighthouse keepers were required after 1872 to post a daily log in a legal-size ledger with marbled cover, supplied to them by the Lighthouse Board. This task obviously required the ability to read and write. Although earlier keepers (both men and women) were expected to maintain simple accounts, their educational qualifications were not a major factor in employment. Keeping the light involved mostly manual labor.

Pages from keeper's log at St. Mark's Light, Florida. The top half written by Charles Fine; the bottom half by his wife, Sarah Fine, who kept the light and the log following her husband's death in June 1904. Courtesy of the National Archives.

Instructions for keeping the log were pasted on the inside of the front cover. [See replica which follows, taken from the front of a log.] Many of the logs for the two decades after 1872, including those kept by women, are now on file in the National Archives in Suitland, Maryland, just outside the District of Columbia.

Keepers interpreted the instructions in different ways. Most of them recorded little more than the weather. Others included details about cleaning and repairing the station. Others identified every ship that passed, or every

8. KEEPERS' LOGS cont.

supply boat that arrived and how long it stayed. They often mentioned visitors to the station. Some included personal information, such as illness, times when the keeper was away from the station, whether school was held, Sunday church services and funerals. A few gave information about domestic animals (cows, chickens, and the like). Some keepers filled in a page of accounts at the end of each month.

All of them recorded disasters such as a long boat foundering, a ship going aground, a seaman drowning. A few added mishaps such as a cellar flooding or machinery breaking down. Some pasted newspaper clippings in their log or inserted letters between the pages. Some keepers wrote their names at the top or bottom of every log page. Others never identified themselves in the log, making it difficult to ascertain who the keeper was or whether the keeper was male or female.

Sarah Fine, who kept St. Marks Light in Florida from 1904 to 1919, did not write her name on every page. Her handwriting and her name appear, however, on June 18, 1904, under the last half-page of her husband's entries, but without any explanation of what happened to him.

Some of the entries in logs kept by women are tantalizingly ambiguous. One mentions an "abusive asst. keeper, being under the influence of liquer [sic]," but doesn't tell us how she coped.

Among the many logs kept by women, that of Harriet Colfax, keeper of the Michigan City Light on Lake Michigan from 1861 to 1904, is one of the most interesting. Her fine hand and excellent grammar are of a higher quality than that found in logs kept by most of the other women, indicating a better-than-average education in the 1830s, when Harriet would have been in school. The significant entries in her log over a 20-year period make her station and her work come alive.

Journal

(1) The events of the day must be written on the same line across both pages and as a general rule, if carefully written, one line will be sufficient for a day's entries. One line must be left blank between each two days. The entries for each month must commence on a new page and on each Sunday the name of the day shall be written in the column for the month, in front of its proper date.

(2) The following entries shall be made in the Journal, viz:

Visits of Inspector, Engineer, Lampist, Machinist or any authorized person; a general account of all work going on at the station by the keepers or others; delivery of supplies; any item of official interest occurring at the station or in its vicinity; any unusual condition of wind or weather with abnormal readings of barometer or thermometer (ordinary conditions of wind or weather with ordinary readings of barometer and thermometer shall be entered only in the Expenditure Book). Where no Watch Book is kept, the fact whether or not all station lights which should be visible from a station are lighted shall be entered in the Journal. A list of such lights shall be entered on the first page of the Journal and it will then be necessary only to state in the remarks for each day: "All lights visible" or "All lights except _____ visible."

(3) No personal opinions or remarks on family affairs or ordinary household work shall be entered in the Journal. All entries must be confined to the subjects enumerated above, the Keeper using his judgment as to what occurrences are of sufficient importance, or official interest to warrant an entry in the Journal.

(4) If visitors are frequently at the station, the entry should be made as follows, viz: "A number of visitors from _____ at station today." or "A party of visitors from _____ at station today." At outlying stations where visitors are infrequent, the names of the visitors or the more prominent ones of the party, if large, should be noted, as well as the place from which they come, etc. The names of all persons (whether officials, workmen or visitors) remaining over night at any station, must be entered at the beginning and end of their visit.

(5) The times of leaving and returning to station of all Keepers shall be entered in the Journal and in cases where there is but one keeper, the name of the person left in charge of the station must be entered.

(6) The keeper shall make a general inspection of his station, light and fog-signal every Saturday and enter this fact, with the condition of the station, light and fog signal in the Journal. If anything prevents the Keeper from making this inspection on Saturday, the fact must be entered in the Journal and the inspection made as soon as practicable and entered in the Journal under the date made.

A 1914 view of Michigan City Light Station at Michigan City, Indiana, kept by Harriet Colfax from 1861 until 1904. No longer supporting an active aid to navigation, the station house now serves as a museum. Courtesy of the National Archives, #26-LG-56-30.

IX. Harriet Colfax at Michigan City Light, Indiana, 1861-1904

The short coast of the state of Indiana along Lake Michigan has at Michigan City a historic light which guided Great Lakes mariners for more than a hundred years. Its history began in 1835, when the founder of Michigan City deeded to the United States government a tract of land running from the bend of Trail Creek to the lake for the express purpose of constructing a lighthouse.

The first light was hung on a tall post located slightly west of the present lighthouse. The first lighthouse was built in 1837—a keeper's dwelling with a 40-foot-high white-washed tower topped with a lantern to house the light. The first keeper was paid $350 a year. The second was a woman, Mrs. Harriet C. Towner, about whom almost nothing is known.

As the shipping of grain and lumber increased, a brighter light was needed to guide the ships. In 1858 the U.S. government constructed a new lighthouse on the shore, using joliet stone for the foundation and Milwaukee brick for the superstructure. The 1858 date can still be seen on the south wall. On the north end of the lighthouse was the lantern which housed a fixed light with a Fresnel lens of the fifth order, visible for 15 miles. Sperm oil was used as fuel in the early years, with a switch to lard oil when it was discovered to be cleaner, and finally to kerosene when it became cheaper than lard oil.

A Mr. Clarkson served as first keeper of the new light. He was replaced in 1861 by Miss Harriet Colfax. In the 19th century, when aids to navigation were the responsibility of the Treasury Department, many lighthouse keepers were political appointees. Miss Colfax's appointment may have been arranged by her cousin, Schuyler Colfax, who was then a member of Congress and later became Vice President when General U. S. Grant became President in 1869. Harriet Colfax had been a teacher of voice and piano in her hometown, Ogdensburg, New

York, but moved to Michigan City in the 1850s with her brother, who founded and published the only local newspaper for many years. Harriet worked as typesetter on the paper, as well as teaching music. There were rumors of a romance gone awry. Then Harriet formed a close friendship with Miss Ann C. Hartwell, also a native of Ogdensburg, who had moved to Indiana to teach school. The two spent the rest of their lives together.

When failing health led her brother to sell the *Transcript* and seek a healthier climate, Harriet stayed on in Michigan City. She was 37 when she took up the lighthouse keeper's appointment in 1861, at an initial salary of $350 a year. Critics of the political influence that won her appointment mentioned her petite size and seeming fragility, but Harriet performed her duties without fail for 43 years, retiring in 1904 at age 80 because of failing health. She died a year later, shortly after Ann Hartwell's death.

A few events of her first decade keeping the lighthouse on the Lake Michigan shore can be gleaned from the annual reports of the Lighthouse Board. The 1868 report said that "the dwelling leaks badly where the tower joins the roof; eaves troughs and conductors are needed; the roof required repairs, and a cistern and new outbuildings are wanted." Repairs were made the next year.

Piers guarded both sides of the entrance to Michigan City Harbor. On November 20, 1871, a beacon light and elevated walk were installed on the east pier, which extended 1,500 feet into Lake Michigan. This light too had to be maintained by the keeper of the shore light.

A year later all keepers began keeping their journals. Harriet Colfax's log is in the National Archives. Her crisp record of her daily activities gives a very vivid picture of her life at the Michigan City Light.

August 12, 1872: Clear & Warm, with light E. Winds. U.S. Tender Haze came in about 5 a.m. with supplies for the St[ation] House. Commodore Murray, St. House Inspector, called at the St. House. Expressed himself satisfied with everything about the establishment.

August 16, 1872: This is the day on which the Comet was to strike the Earth and demolish all things terrestrial—but failed to come up to appointment. The elevated walk [on the east pier] was run into by a Vessel entering the harbor & considerably damaged. 5 [ship] arrivals.

Damage to the elevated walkway was reported several times a year by Miss Colfax. This walkway was a wooden structure raised to some height above the pier on metal struts, allowing a pedestrian to reach the end of the pier when stormy water swept over the pier. Many moments of real danger were associated with that walkway.

September 18, 1872: Cold day. Heavy N. W. gale towards night. The waves dashing over both Piers, very nearly carrying me with them into the lake.

Some vivid images can be drawn from this cryptic entry. Miss Colfax probably did not wear trousers, nor did she have yellow slickers to keep her dry. She may have worn an oilskin coat over her long dress, but her heavy skirts must have dragged

A later pier at Michigan City Light in rough weather. The light keeper walked out on this type of elevated walkway to light the beacon at the end. Courtesy of the National Archives, #26-LG-56-32.

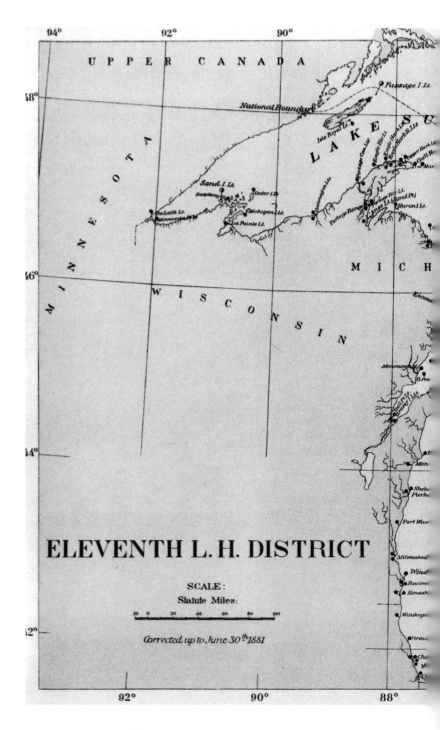

ELEVENTH L. H. DISTRICT

SCALE:

Statute Miles:

Corrected up to June 30th 1881

1881 Annual Report of the Lighthouse Board.

around her ankles as they got wet. Freezing weather made the footing slippery. In cold weather the lard oil to fuel the beacon had to be heated to keep it from solidifying. If she was delayed waiting for high waves to pass and too much time elapsed in reaching the beacon, the oil congealed and would not ignite, forcing her to return to the station house and reheat it. The storms she described buffeted her with wild gusts of wind, flinging not only waves across the walkway, but also blinding sheets of spray and sleet. When her task was finally completed, her soaked clothes would have been hung to dry by the wood stove. She would have no hot shower to revive her.

Barely ten days later, *September 29: Wind blowing a westerly gale all day & still rising at 5 p.m. Four vessels entered while the gale was at its height & ran against the elevated walk, breaking it in again. Went to the beacon tonight with considerable risk of life.*

The next day she mentioned that "the sails of the vessels which entered in yesterday's storm were hanging in shreds, but no other injuries sustained." A month later (November 7) in another storm, a vessel went ashore east of the piers. The next day's entry: *The Sch[ooner] Scotland went to pieces and sank in the night. Gathered the particulars of the wreck & reported the same to Com. Murray at Detroit—St. H. Inspector. The Gale of yesterday continued unabated. 1 arrival.*

Storms and nasty weather characterized Lake Michigan as winter set in. *November 19, 1872: Terrible day. Wind blowing a northerly gale—snowing & drifting. Crossing good on the ice [of the frozen harbor]. Looks as tho' Winter was fairly upon us, & a few days at the farthest would close up navigation. The* City of Tawas *has made her last trip & will go into Winter quarters here. Other vessels reported in Chicago papers following suit—also a good many wrecks, with fearful loss of life.*

Similar entries continued until *December 8: A terrible Northwesterly gale & snow storm. Growing cold very rapidly. Ice driven back into the creek & uniting permanently for the Winter this time, to all appearances. 3 p.m.: Storm increasing— Snow swirling & drifting. The most terrific gale & snow storm of the season. I exhibited the Lights to-night as I never close up in a storm, but it is probably for the last time this season.*

December 13: Put the lamps, etc. away for the Winter, covered from dust & dampness. (In December of another year

Michigan City Lt. Station,
December 31, 1900.

U.S. Lt. House Inspector,
    9th. Lt. House District,
        Chicago, Ill.,

Sir:—
        I have to report depth of water at
Entrance to harbor—   24 ft. 9"
Lt.S. Station —   16 "
First bend in Creek —   16 . 9"
Franklin-St. bridge —   14 . 2"
M. C. R.R. bridge —   17 . 3"

        Vessels on entering the harbor
should keep from 30 ft. to 40 ft. from the
breakwater pier — which is the pier on
the starboard side — and center of channel
to bend.
        Very Respectfully,
                Harriet E. Colfax,
                    Lt. Keeper

Letter from Harriet Colfax to the Lighthouse Inspector, dated November 31, 1900. Found inserted between the pages of the log she kept. Courtesy of the National Archives.

she wrote that this end-of-season ritual included cleaning and polishing the lamps, wrapping up the lens in cotton batting and kerosene, storing all the parts in the oil house, and washing the glass and painted surfaces in the lantern.)

During the months when the harbor was closed, Miss Colfax recorded only the weather. Shipping resumed the following May, when a log entry mentioned that she had requested a 130-foot extension to the elevated walk to the beacon. She justified the need for the extension barely two weeks later. *May 28, 1873: A terrible hurricane to-night at about the time of lighting up [the beacon]. Narrowly escaped being swept into the lake.*

When summer weather made her post more attractive, her entries mention "large numbers of visitors [came from the town] to see the lamps." Ships entering the harbor brought visitors as well.

August 17, 1873: The Supply Vessel Haze *put in (as usual) a very unexpected appearance this morning about 7 o'clock. Commodore Murray, St. H. Inspector, Captain Davis of the St. H. Board & Col. Wilkins, U.S.A., were aboard & came up to the house. The Officers expressed themselves much pleased with the buildings, lanterns, light, apparatus, etc. 2 arrivals. Obtained Com. Murray's approval of the extension of the elevated walk up to the beach line & also of a plank walk extending from the St. H. to the pier.*

By August 26 the extension had been completed, the walk laid, and a new floor put in the kitchen. But the walk extension did not remove all the difficulties of keeping the beacon lighted. *October 28, 1873: Terrific westerly gale. The waves dashing high over both piers, & over my head when on my way down to light the beacon. October 31: Mainlight and Beacon both bewitched tonight, requiring my constant attention during the entire night.*

The fall of 1874 began inauspiciously: *September 9: Man lost overboard from Schr. Herald.* In October the Lighthouse Board informed Harriet that the beacon was to be moved to the west pier, which extended 500 feet further into the lake than the east pier. This would require the keeper to cross the creek by boat, walk along the other side of the creek, ascend the elevated walkway, climb the beacon ladder, and light the light. Work on moving the elevated walk from the east to the west

Harriet Colfax, keeper of the Michigan City Light in Michigan City, Indiana, from 1861 until 1904. Courtesy of the Old Lighthouse Museum, Michigan City Historical Society, Inc.

pier was interrupted by a northeasterly gale. The mechanical pile driver and engine supporting the work were carried away in the storm.

On October 20 Miss Colfax petitioned the Lighthouse Board to give her an assistant to tend the beacon. On October 29 she wrote that, because the elevated walkway had been removed, a gale kept her from reaching the beacon in the morning to extinguish the light. Not until November 16 was the walk completed and the beacon moved, but mariners were not yet apprised of the change. *November 20: The Schr.* Rowens *came ashore outside the W. pier this night in consequence of the removal of the Light—will be a wreck.*

Apparently Miss Colfax's request for an assistant was granted. *November 23: The man in temporary charge of the Beacon Light was unable to reach it tonight—consequently the Light was not exhibited. Storm increasing in fury when the Sun went down.*

The next day part of the elevated walkway was carried away and the beacon again unlighted.

Harriet recorded these kinds of damaging storms every year. *December 5, 1885: Gale continues, with snow—cold. Elevated walk badly damaged & beacon light damaged and put out. The beacon cannot be repaired this fall. Telegraphed Inspector & afterwards wrote him & the Engineer. Telegram from Insp'tor to "hang a lantern out," which I did.*

The next night the beacon was carried away in the storm. The following two nights Harriet sent a man in a tug to light the beacon, for there was no other way to reach it. The next day she asked permission to use the tug the rest of the season. Two days later she was told to close the lights as soon as possible, which she did the following day. In March the Inspector made her re-explain the causes of the darkened beacon and the need for a tug to light it.

In March of 1886 the entire superstructure on the west pier was carried away by a storm. The beacon was not replaced by a temporary light until June. In October the temporary light and the beacon structure were both carried away and thrown up onto the beach.

Every month Harriet mentioned preparing a monthly report, four times a year a quarterly report, and every winter an annual report to send to the Lighthouse Board. She recorded her various leaves of absence once she had an assistant to care for the station. In 1876 she visited the Centennial Exposition in Philadelphia. In the summer of 1882 she visited friends in Terre Haute for two weeks, and spent the Christmas holidays in Terre Haute and St. Louis. In 1885 she visited her brother in Wyandotte, Michigan; in 1886 spent the Christmas holiday with her sister. In 1887 she requested leave throughout the entire winter when the lights were closed.

Many of her entries had a simple domestic quality to them. In May of 1879 she noted that she had sewn rings on lantern curtains for the beacon. The curtains were hung around the lamps in the daytime to keep the sun from spontaneously combusting the oil. Repeated entries mention cleaning and polishing the lamps and shining the brass. Other notations give glimpses of life in the station house. She writes almost every year of painting the stairs and floors and having the station house and the oil house painted. (Normally keepers were required to do all such painting, but women were exempted from painting whole buildings.) The paint could not have been very durable because once she mentioned the rain washing off the black paint that had just been applied to the lantern.

Every spring much of the sand that had washed into the yard during the winter had to be removed and the yard graded. Twice Harriet wrote that soot in the wood stove chimney caught fire, "causing quite a fright." Each fall she received a check ($20 to $30) for wood to heat her house. The Lighthouse Board continued to pay for wood until 1882, when they informed Miss Colfax that she would have to pay for her own thereafter.

This sounds petty, but the keeper's small salary was augmented by free housing and many staples (delivered periodically by lighthouse tender) on which to live. In 1882 the keeper's allowance included 200 pounds of pork, 100 pounds of beef, 50 pounds of sugar, 2 barrels of flour, 24 pounds of coffee, 10 gallons of beans, 4 gallons of vinegar, 2 barrels of potatoes, 50 pounds of rice, and 13 ounces of mustard and pepper. The large amount of vinegar may have been for disinfecting purposes, but why no salt?

In August of 1882 Harriet had trouble with a leaking lamp reservoir, and requested that the Lighthouse Board lampist come to fix it. She was told to switch lamps until he arrived. That same year several entries pertain to attempts to sink a tube well and find a steady supply of water. Finally she was authorized to spend $15 having an ordinary well dug. One of the tantalizing entries refers to repairs to the water closet, and then to having the outside of the water closet and lattices painted. She was obviously describing an outhouse.

She wrote of seeing a mirage from the lantern, of a total eclipse of the moon, of a double rainbow, of hailstorms, of glorious displays of Northern Lights. She recorded the day

President Garfield was shot, and that she draped the station house in mourning when he died in 1881, and again when President Grant and Vice President Hendricks died in 1885. She mentions her confusion over an order from the Lighthouse Board outlining the official uniform she was supposed to wear (double-breasted coat with yellow buttons, dark blue trousers, and a cap bearing a yellow metal lighthouse badge). The inspector assured her that "women keepers were exempted" from this order.

Local deaths were recorded—the drowning of three fishermen after their boat capsized, a schooner captain struck by an engine, another drowned ten miles away from her lighthouse. In 1885 the lighthouse keeper at Racine, Wisconsin, drowned in a storm. In 1886 a barge mate in her own harbor was struck in the head by a heavy log and killed.

Shipments of oil, wick, lamps, and other supplies were received and acknowledged. In 1882 instructions from the Station House Engineer told her to clean and polish all the lard oil lamps in preparation for exchanging them for kerosene (known as mineral oil) lamps. Occasionally she was asked to ship surplus oil to a neighboring light station.

One of the most surprising requests to come from the Inspector was an instruction to "find out all about the birds and insects in this vicinity." Harriet noted that this was beyond her depth, so she "turned the letter over to the resident taxidurmist [sic]." A follow-up inquiry asked about bird migrations.

The Lighthouse Board must have been cramped for finances in 1882, for the assistant's position at the Michigan City Light was revoked. Harriet, then 58 years old, wrote letters all winter asking for help in tending the beacon. She kept both lights by herself through the following summer, and finally received permission in September to reemploy Mr. James, her former assistant. The following year he was demoted to the status of "laborer." In April 1885 a new assistant keeper, Mr. Timothy Fogarty, was appointed, but no explanation of the switch is given. In 1888 the Lighthouse Board reduced Miss Colfax's salary from $600 annually to $540. Again, no explanation is given, nor did Harriet record any judgments. If dealing with the lighthouse bureaucracy in Detroit gave her problems, she never indicated it. Her log entries were all factual and objectively phrased.

In 1892 the Lighthouse Board reported that "a number of persons have occupied the light-house grounds without authority. Measures have been taken to cause them to remove their shanties and other property." In 1894 an 83-foot-deep well was sunk, ending the fresh water problem. Every annual report for the rest of the decade recommended the addition of a fog signal to the station. Its construction was undertaken in 1904, and coincided with Miss Colfax's retirement.

Upon retirement, Harriet followed the last of the many instructions in *Instructions to Light-Keepers*: "When a keeper resigns or is removed, a correct inventory of all public property under his charge must be made in the presence of his successor . . . No keeper who resigns or is removed, and no representative of such keeper, shall receive any balance on account of salary until he shall have accounted satisfactorily for all public property in his charge."[24]

October 6, 1904: Commenced taking inventory of public property. On October 8: Sold household effects preparatory to vacating dear old St. House. October 11: The new Keeper arrived today and made pleasant call at St. House. Miss Colfax's last entry in the official log was on October 12. She died five months later, at age 80.

The dwelling which continued to serve as the keeper's living quarters was remodeled in 1904, after Miss Colfax's retirement, and enlarged by adding two rooms to each floor on the north side. This resulted in duplex apartments, the keeper and his family using all three floors on the east and the assistant keeper those on the west. The lantern along with its fifth order fresnel lens was moved from the house to the new fog signal lighthouse on the east pier at the entrance of Michigan City's harbor. In 1933 the light on the east pier was electrified. Three women—Abigail Coit, Julia Ebart, and Katy Reilly—served as assistant keepers in the years before the Coast Guard assumed responsibility for the Michigan City East Pierhead Light.

In the 1960s, the East Pierhead Light was automated and the City of Michigan City purchased the keeper's house and established a museum in it. A replica of the original lantern tower was placed on the roof in 1973.[25]

Calumet Harbor Light on Lake Michigan just east of Chicago in 1914. Courtesy of the National Archives, #26-LG-55-13.

X. Mary Ryan at Calumet Harbor Entrance Light, Indiana, 1873-1880

Temperament was a important ingredient in a successful lighthouse keeper, particularly in an isolated location. Not all women keepers reacted to their assignments with the equanimity of Harriet Colfax. Mary Ryan, who kept the Calumet Harbor Entrance Light in Indiana (located offshore on a pier) from 1873 to 1880 after her husband died, expressed her dislike of her post in no uncertain terms.

December 25, 1873: I was suppose [sic] to have been informed when this light would be discontinued [for the winter], not a vessel since the 15th of Nov. and nothing to light for and this is such a dreary place to be in all alone.

April 7, 1874: Oh, for a home in the sunny south, such a climate.

April 16: Such a time, everyone is despaired thinking that summer is never coming.

May 1: So cold, Mayday!, those people who go for flowers will be disappointed.

May 2: Nothing but gloom, without and WITHIN.

October 31: A promise of a cold hard winter as the signs show, so many out of employment at this early in the season, and what will it be before winter is over? God "only knows."

April 22, 1880: I think some changes will have to be made, this is not a fit place for anyone to live in.

July 31: This has been the most trying month of my keeping a lighthouse, the most important question, can anything worse come?

August 28: The lighthouse engineers never do anything for me.

August 30: Oh what a place.

November 1: This is all gloom and darkness.[26]

Mary Ryan was doubtless very pleased when her replacement arrived in 1880.

Santa Barbara Light Station in California was first lighted in 1856. Julia Williams was keeper from 1865 to 1905; Caroline Morse from 1905 to 1911. The lighthouse was later demolished in the 1925 earthquake. Courtesy of the U.S. Coast Guard.

Julia Williams and Caroline Morse

XI. Julia Williams, 1865-1905, and Caroline Morse, 1905-1911, at Santa Barbara Light, California

The discovery of gold in California in 1848 led to rapid growth of ports on the Pacific Coast. The Santa Barbara channel was particularly hazardous for early mariners because ships must make a 90-degree turn to round the land's sharp thrust out to sea. The nine Santa Barbara Islands lie just to the south. Before the Santa Barbara lighthouse was erected in 1856, the channel had been a graveyard for ships.

Albert Johnson Williams, originally from Kennebec, Maine, took his family to California in 1850. In 1856 they traveled by horse and oxcart to Santa Barbara to occupy the barely completed lighthouse (built in the uniform Cape Cod style popular in the 1850s) before there was even a road from the town to the mesa on which it stood. Santa Barbara was so small in those days that Mrs. Williams could invite all the 30 Americans in the town to a Christmas dinner at the lighthouse in 1857. This would have been a major social occasion for women whose contacts with other women and their families were limited by distance and cumbersome transportation.

A Williams baby was born in the lighthouse two months before the three lamps were first displayed in the lantern. In 1904 this child, named Bion, wrote an entertaining account of those early days, entitled "The Santa Barbara Light and its Keeper."

The isolation of the lighthouse in his childhood provided many challenges. Bion's father had another job in town, leaving his mother very much on her own. Women who went west in the mid-19th century had to perform a multitude of domestic tasks. Fresh water was to be caught in a cistern, but rain seldom fell. Mrs. Williams saddled a horse, took the baby in her arms, and, followed by two little girls, rode a mile to a spring to bring home cans of water slung to the saddle. She gathered wood for her cook stove in the same manner. She did her own sewing and mending. Many years later her grandson remembered particularly the excellent fresh-baked bread Mrs. Williams gave him, and the masses of orange and yellow nasturtiums blooming in the lighthouse yard.

In the early days all supplies came to the few stores in nearby Santa Barbara in small sailing vessels, arriving every month or two. When something ran out, customers waited for the next ship. Without even a right of way to the lighthouse until 1877, getting to town to fetch supplies was a challenge in itself. Mission Creek ran between the lighthouse and the town and had to be waded. On those rare occasions when rain flooded the creek, the crossing was perilous.

Through some misunderstanding, another keeper was sent to the light in 1860, and the Williams family retreated to a recently acquired ranch nearby. The new keeper stayed only briefly, but Mr. Williams was tired of the monotony of lighthouse routine, and sent his hired man every night to light the lamp. In 1865 his wife agreed to tend the light at a salary of $750 a year. She had produced another baby in the interim, and bore two more in 1866 and 1869. Mr. Williams continued ranching until his death in 1882.

Gradually the countryside was changing, with farms being fenced off and houses built. The Williams's son Frank grew corn and beans on the surrounding land and became a prosperous farmer. His brother Albert grazed dairy cows. In 1868 the *Annual Report of the Lighthouse Board* stated that "extensive repairs have been made at this station. In the cellar a new floor has been made of bricks laid on edge in cement, in place of the old floor, which, being composed of bricks laid flat in ordinary mortar, was flooded by heavy rains. A drain leading outside from the cellar has also been constructed. A brick chimney has been substituted for the stove-pipe which passed through the roof and was considered unsafe. The tower and chimneys, where they pass through the roof, have been repointed with cement mortar. A storm-house has been built over and in front of the kitchen door, to keep out the rain." In 1880 mineral oil replaced lard oil in the lamps. In 1881 "the roadway leading from the reservation to the county road was improved and repaired;" in 1893 a 50-foot well sunk; in 1894 a "galvanized

Office of Light-House Inspector,

TWELFTH DISTRICT.

San Francisco, Cal. *March 10th, 1875*

Mrs Julia Williams
Keeper Santa Barbara Lt Station

Madam,

You will please send immediately to this Office a list of Supplies required for Station under your charge for year commencing July 1st 1875.

Please read pages 156 to 169 "Organization and Duties of Light-House Board. 1871" before making requisition.

State quantity of Oil on hand at date of your letter: also quantity of Coal and Wood.

Are you allowed Rations and Fuel?

Respectfully &c

S. T. Snell
Comdr W. S. N
Inspector —

Letter dated March 10, 1875, from the Lighthouse Inspector to Julia Williams, keeper of Santa Barbara Light Station, California. Inserted between the pages of the log she kept. Courtesy of the National Archives.

iron windmill was erected on a steel spider tower over the well dug last year." The station received a new fourth order lens in 1898.

Julia Williams, keeper of the Santa Barbara Light, California, 1865-1905. Courtesy of the Santa Barbara Historical Society.

Mrs. Williams retired in 1905, at age 80. In 1911 a local newspaper printed the following obituary:

> Mrs. Julia F. Williams, who for forty years was keeper of the Santa Barbara lighthouse, died Friday night at the Cottage hospital where she had been a patient sufferer since her fall [which broke her hip] at the lighthouse six years ago.
>
> "The Lighthouse Lady," a title won by years of faithful service, was known to every naval officer and coasting captain that crossed the Channel. She was identified with the pioneer history of this city, being the first American woman in the presidio of Santa Barbara, and her memory was a veritable mine of early events. Her life of faithful service made hers one of the most historic and picturesque careers of the Pacific coast.
>
> . . . Mrs. Williams was . . . at the time of her retirement the oldest incumbent in the lighthouse service.
>
> In the forty years of service she was never out of sight of the house after dark. Every night she climbed the three flights of stairs at sunset and lighted the lamp. Every night at midnight the lamp was trimmed or changed for a fresh one, and every morning as the sun touched the mountain tops the same hand extinguished the light and drew the curtain across the lens and went about her household duties.
>
> There were no fog signals and only one keeper, but there was only one wreck and that occurred one beautiful moonlight night when the careless captain allowed his vessel *The Pride of the Sea*, laden with merchandise, to drift too near the shore and was unable to keep off the rocks. . . .[27]

Julia Williams was succeeded at the Santa Barbara Light Station by Caroline Morse, who was keeper from 1905 to 1911, but details of her tenure are not available. The lighthouse was demolished in the earthquake of 1925 and replaced with an acetylene-powered light on a wooden tower.

Postcard from around the turn of the century of the reconstructed Sand Point Light at Escanaba, Michigan. Mary Terry kept this light from 1868 to 1886, when she died in a fire which destroyed the lighthouse. Courtesy of the Delta County Historical Society.

XII. Mary Terry at Sand Point Light, Michigan, 1868-1886

Mary Terry's husband John was appointed the first keeper of the new lighthouse on Sand Point at Escanaba, Michigan, while it was still under construction. The couple moved from St. Catherines, Ontario, Canada, to Escanaba in 1867. John died of consumption before the lighthouse was completed. The citizens of Escanaba recommended that his wife replace him. Local government officials strongly opposed the idea, but Mary received the official appointment in 1868 and began the operation of the new light.

She apparently met the challenge. The Escanaba *Iron Port* reported that "she was a very methodical woman, very careful in the discharge of her duties and very particular in the care of the property under her charge." Mrs. Terry maintained the light on Lake Michigan's cold and windy northern shore for almost 18 years, using a wood furnace to keep warm in winter. In March of 1886 the handyman who helped Mrs. Terry with maintenance noticed that the wood near the furnace was hot. When he called the keeper's attention to it, she replied that she expected to be burned out one day, but added that she slept with one eye open.

Her premonition materialized during the following night, when fire destroyed the lighthouse. "When the alarm was given, at about one o'clock, the flames had entire possession of the building and had broken through the roof, and nothing could be done either to save it or its contents. It was known that the keeper Mrs. Mary L. Terry, occupied the building, and as she was not seen or heard from, it was at once apprehended that she perished in the house, and when the subsidence of the fire and the coming of daylight made an examination of the ruins possible, these fears were changed to certainties by the discovery of her remains therein.

"Justice Glaser and a coroner's jury . . . viewed the remains (mere fragments—a portion of the skull, a few bones, and a small portion of the viscera), which were then placed in charge of D. A. Oliver and an adjournment taken to give time for the collection of evidence. The furnace by which the house was heated was in bad order, and it is not impossible the fire originated there."[28]

Those who knew Mary Terry had difficulty believing that someone so efficient could have died by accident or her own carelessness. The fact that her remains were found in the oilroom in the southwest corner of the lighthouse, and not in her bedroom on the northeast side of the house, led some to speculate that she was the victim of murder, robbery, and arson. At age 69 she was reputed to be a woman of means, who had several thousand dollars in a savings account and had purchased several valuable building lots in the city.

The verdict of the coroner's jury a week later "that Mrs. Terry came to her death from causes and by means to the jury unknown was," according to the March 13 issue of the *Iron Port*, "the only one that could be rendered. There was and is a general feeling of suspicion, based on Mrs. Terry's known cool headedness, that she did not come to her end accidentally, and this feeling is strengthened by the fact that the south door was found open and that the lock was found with the bolt shot forward as though the door had been forced, not unlocked, but the theory of robbery does not find support in the fact that money, gold pieces, were found where they would have fallen from the cupboard, the place where she usually kept what she kept in the house, and that a bundle of papers, insurance policy, deeds, etc., charred throughout but preserving its form sufficiently to show what it had been, was also found.

"The verdict, then, was the only one possible, and the truth of the affair can never be known. There may have been foul play, but there is no evidence to justify an assertion that there was; no circumstances that are not consistent with a theory of accidental death."[29]

XIII. Nancy Rose at Stony Point Light, New York, 1871-1904

Our picture of Mrs. Nancy Rose comes from an article published in the *New York Tribune* on June 28, 1903, shortly before she was preparing to retire. Her intention was to move from the lighthouse high above the Hudson River on the crest of Stony Point to a cottage being built just behind the railroad station in the village at the base of the mountain.

The first keeper at Stony Point was Robert Parkinson, Nancy Rose's uncle, appointed in 1825. According to the *Tribune*, Nancy's husband, Alexander Rose, became the second keeper in the spring of 1852. A few years later, while carrying timbers for the bell tower which the government was then constructing, he ruptured a blood vessel and died a few weeks later. After his death his wife took over his duties, trimming the lights and keeping the fogbell going from one end of the year to the next, for the Hudson River is often open to navigation throughout the winter. The *Tribune* said that Nancy Rose had lived on the height for 50 years, 47 of them as official keeper, with sole responsibility for the point's two beacon lights and fogbell. Thus her tenure as keeper would have started in 1856, although her name does not appear as official keeper in "Lighthouse Keepers and Assistants" until 1871.

The newspaper article was written when Nancy was then 79 and still in fine health, but she indicated to the *Tribune* reporter that she no longer found lighthouse tending as satisfying as it had seemed to her when, as a young widow and the mother of six small children, she took up her husband's duties.

The lighthouse on Stony Point was built in 1826 on the foundation of Stony Point Fort, the old walls having long since been filled in to become a terrace of grass and shrubs. The Rose family frequently found old bullets and grapeshot, rusty and soil-eaten, around the fort. A flagpole marked the spot where

Mad Anthony Wayne, of Revolutionary War fame, was supposed to have fallen. Mrs. Rose's great-grandfather, Jacob Parkinson, was wounded in the same battle.

From the little balcony around the lantern one could see for miles up and down the Hudson River. The rolling hills followed its course, blue and misty as they melted away to the horizon. The trim little cottage on the mountain top was surrounded with climbing roses and old-fashioned shrubs. Nancy Rose kept the interior immaculate.

In bad weather the fog machinery had to be wound up every three and three-quarters hours, and the lighthouse lamps replenished every midnight. In 1880 the fogbell was removed from the lighthouse at the top of the hill to a spot nearer the water and further away from the house, requiring the keeper to hike back and forth to the site whenever fog closed in. In 1902 a red lens lantern was placed on top of the belltower near the water, again increasing the keeper's duties, for it had to be trimmed and tended nightly. Nancy Rose's salary remained the same throughout, however—$500 a year.

Mrs. Rose never left the station without notifying the inspector of her intended absence. She also recorded weather conditions every day, along with the time of lighting and extinguishing the lamps, and the disposal of every ounce of supplies and inch of wick. The lighthouse inspector came unheralded in his tender at uncertain intervals, bringing supplies and making routine inspections of the five hundred aids to navigation in his district. He went over the entire premises, even the garret, cellar, and barn, but no criticism of Nancy Rose's lighthouse was ever recorded.

The *Tribune* reporter also found everything about Stony Point Light "exquisitely clean. A new coat of gray paint has just made the woodwork resplendent, and the copper floor of the light chamber is burnished like gold. There is even a great canvas hood, with which the huge refracting lenses are covered during the day to keep any speck of dust from the polished metal and glass."

Only two of Nancy's six children survived—Melinda and Alexander—both of whom lived with their mother. Boredom seems to have played some part in the family's decision to leave the lighthouse. Stony Point provided little of the excitement described by some of the other women keepers at busier spots.

"You must have had many interesting experiences?" Mrs. Rose was asked by the reporter.

"No," was the answer. "Nothing ever happens up here. One year is exactly like another, and except for the weather, nothing changes."

Alexander, Jr., who was at the time supervisor of the little village of Stony Point, was asked if he would like to tend the light after his mother gave up the appointment. His emphatic reply: "Not much. I'd rather pick huckleberries over the mountain for a living."

Melinda's reaction was much the same. "I can't remember anything that has ever happened, except once our cow died,

Stony Point Light on the Hudson River, kept by Nancy Rose from 1871 until 1904. The 1826 tower is now in a state park. Courtesy of the National Archives, #26-LG-17-1.

and several times it's been bad years for the chickens. But even the one wreck wasn't really what you might call a wreck, for nobody was hurt, and it wasn't mother's fault anyhow, for both the lights were burning as brightly as ever."

The wreck which was the highlight of their sojourn at Stony Point occurred in 1901, between 1 and 2 a.m. on a windy, rainy March morning, when the *Poughkeepsie*, a Central Hudson Steamboat Company passenger ship, went aground. Mrs. Rose had just returned from her nightly visit to the lighthouse and was changing her storm-soaked clothes when a pounding on her door startled her. Outside forty or fifty persons, among them seven women, sought shelter from the storm. The Roses did what they could, building a roaring fire in the kitchen stove to dry shoes and garments and dispensing hot coffee until the next train to New York was due.

Some of the Roses' disenchantment with the lighthouse may have resulted from the creation of a state park on Stony Point. After it opened, the lighthouse grounds were overrun in summer months with picnickers and sightseers who wanted to tour the whole place, including the tower.

Official instructions about visitors at light stations were very specific. "Keepers must be courteous and polite to all visitors and show them everything of interest about the station at such times as will not interfere with light-house duties. Keepers must not allow visitors to handle the apparatus or deface light-house property. Special care must be taken to prevent the scratching of names or initials on the glass of the lanterns or on the windows of the towers. The keeper on duty at the time is responsible for any injury or defacement to the buildings, lenses, lamps, glazing of the lantern and to any other light-house property under his charge, unless he can identify the parties who have done the injury, so as to make them accountable for it; and any such damage must be reported immediately to the inspector or engineer of the district, with the names of the person or persons, if they can be ascertained. No visitor should be admitted to the tower unless attended by a keeper, nor in the watch room or lantern between sunset and sunrise."[30]

Reaching the lantern in the Stony Point Light involved three sets of steep steps and unlocking doors and trapdoors. Nancy and her children may have found the repeated climbing of the stairs and the supervision of large numbers of park visitors trying.

Nancy Rose apparently never left the lighthouse to live in her new house, for she died in 1904. Her daughter Melinda could not have been completely disenchanted with the Stony Point Station, for she applied to succeed her mother as keeper. Lighthouse keepers had been moved into the Civil Service in 1896. When told that she was too old (53) to qualify under the new rules, Melinda sought the help of her Congressman in having the age requirement waived so she could take the examination and establish her eligibility. She had been assisting her mother for years, and received at least two temporary appointments. Her official appointment is recorded in "Lighthouse Keepers and Assistants" in 1904, but in 1905 she was succeeded by a male keeper.[31]

HARPER'S WEEKLY.

JOURNAL OF CIVILIZATION

VOL. XIII.—No. 657.] NEW YORK, SATURDAY, JULY 31, 1869. [SINGLE COPIES, TEN CENTS. $4.00 PER YEAR IN ADVANCE.

Entered according to Act of Congress, in the Year 1869, by Harper & Brothers, in the Clerk's Office of the District Court of the United States, for the Southern District of New York.

MISS IDA LEWIS, THE HEROINE OF NEWPORT.—PHOT. BY MANCHESTER BROTHERS, PROVIDENCE, R.I.—[SEE PAGE 484.]

Ida Lewis, famous for her daring rescues at Lime Rock Light, was on the cover of Harper's Weekly *in July 1869. Courtesy of the U.S. Coast Guard.*

XIV. Ida Lewis at Lime Rock Light, Rhode Island, 1879-1911

Idawalley Zorada Lewis, called Ida, was born in Newport, Rhode Island, in 1842. Her father, Captain Hosea Lewis, was a coast pilot whose health was declining. In 1853 he became the first keeper of nearby Lime Rock beacon on a tiny island a third of a mile from the shore of Newport. At first there was only a temporary lantern and a rough shed that provided shelter when the keeper was on the island in bad weather. His family remained in the old part of Newport until 1857, when a Greek Revival building with a hip roof was constructed on the island. Lewis moved his family into the lighthouse when Ida, his eldest child, was 15.

A Newport journalist, George Brewerton, writing a feature story about Ida some years later, provides a detailed description of the lighthouse:

> The house itself is a square two-story building, plain even to ugliness, containing a parlor, dining-room and hall, with an L serving as a kitchen below. Above we find three bed-rooms, two large and one small, with a passage way and elevated closet, raised a step or two and reached by a door from the hall, to contain the lamp. Strangers imagine a tower, more or less lofty, . . . and are consequently disappointed . . .. A narrow window, slightly projecting and fitted with glass upon three sides to hold the lamp, is all that the land-locked position of the place requires to fulfill the purpose for which it was erected. Within the bare walls the very humble attempts at furnishing speak of what the middle class might deem comfort, while the more affluent would regard it as indicative of a condition not very far removed from poverty itself.
>
> Ida's own particular sanctum is fitted with a cheaply finished cottage set, only remarkable as exhibiting a rude painting of a sinking wreck upon the head-board of her couch. . . . A sewing machine, a recent acquisition, with

some little feminine nick-nacks, complete the interior, while its two windows, one on either side, command a fine prospect of the harbor, looking toward the town.

Hosea Lewis had been at Lime Rock less than four months when he was stricken by a disabling stroke. Like many wives and daughters of lighthouse keepers before and after, Ida expanded her domestic duties, now increased by the care of her invalid father and a seriously ill sister, to include the care of the light—filling the lamp with oil at sundown and again at midnight, trimming the wick, polishing the carbon off the reflectors, extinguishing the light at dawn. All these responsibilities precluded further formal education for Ida.

Since Lime Rock was completely surrounded by water, the only way to reach the mainland was by boat. In the mid-19th century it was highly unusual for a woman to handle a boat, but Ida, the oldest of four children, rowed her siblings to school every week day and fetched needed supplies from the town. The wooden boat was heavy, but she became very skillful in handling it. (An article in *Harper's Weekly*, written after Ida had made several daring rescues, debated whether it was "feminine" for women to row boats, but concluded that none but a "donkey" would consider it "unfeminine" to save lives.) Ida was also reputed to be the best swimmer in all Newport.

In a newspaper clipping of the time, her father is quoted as saying,

> Again and again I have seen the children from this window as they were returning from school in some heavy blow, when Ida alone was with them, and old sailor that I am, I felt that I would not give a penny for their lives, so furious was the storm. . . . I have watched them till I could not bear to look any longer, expecting any moment to see them swamped, and the crew at the mercy of the waves, and then I have turned away and said to my wife, let me know if they get safe in, for I could not endure to see them perish and realize that we were powerless to save them.

Ida's skill at the oars was regularly tested. During her first year at Lime Rock, four young men who were out sailing nearly drowned. One of them had foolishly shimmied up the mast and rocked the boat to tease his companions. The boat capsized, and four boys who couldn't swim clung to the overturned hull, shouting for help.

Ida heard them and rowed to their rescue. In their terror, they almost dragged her overboard, but she pulled all four over the stern into her boat and returned them to land. This was only the first of a number of rescues which later made Ida famous.

Ida and her mother tended the Lime Rock Light for her father from 1857 until 1872, when he died. Her mother was appointed keeper until 1879, although Ida continued to do the keeper's work. Then Ida received the official appointment and her own salary ($500 a year). She continued at her post until her own death in 1911. On the night of her death the bells on all the vessels anchored in Newport Harbor were tolled in her memory.

Because of her many rescues, Ida Lewis became the best-known lighthouse keeper of her day. During her 39 years on Lime Rock, Ida is credited with saving 18 lives, although unofficial reports suggest the number may have been as high as 25. One such rescue, on March 29, 1869, is immortalized in a

Lime Rock Light Station at Newport harbor, Rhode Island, was kept by Ida Lewis from 1879 to 1911. The station now serves as a yacht club. Courtesy of the U.S. Coast Guard.

painting commissioned by the U.S. Coast Guard. The instructions to the artist noted that Ida Lewis's hair was dark brown and that she always wore a shawl over her shoulders and a "standard brown poplin dress." The instructions also urged the artist to "depict any rescue from the stern as Ida always brought the rescued person in from that location. Any other location would have capsized the boat." The artist was also told to "note the manner in which the oars are shipped," but instead has painted Ida extending one of her oars to the drowning man, while her younger brother Rudolph steadies the boat with his oar. The background of the painting includes a glimpse of the Lime Rock Lighthouse. The artist may have amalgamated details from several rescues into his painting.

Ida's fame spread quickly after the 1869 rescue, for a reporter was sent from the *New York Tribune* to record her deeds. Articles also appeared in *Harper's Weekly*, *Leslie's* magazine, and other leading newspapers. The Life Saving Benevolent Association of New York sent her a silver medal and a check for $100—a substantial sum to a young woman who then earned $600 a year. A parade was held in her honor in Newport on Independence Day, followed by the presentation of a sleek mahogany rowboat with red velvet cushions, gold braid around the gunwales, and gold-plated oarlocks. When she was 64, Ida became a life beneficiary of the Carnegie Hero Fund, receiving a monthly pension of $30.

The Newport journalist, George D. Brewerton, decided to write a pamphlet about her and went out to Lime Rock to seek her assistance. He described his visits in the flowery language of the time:

> In pursuit of this quest we have gone once and again, accompanied by our little boy, a juvenile greatly interested in Ida's dogs, rabbits and other Lime Rock pets, whose gambols served to amuse this lad while his father jotted down his notes at the table. Sitting in the snug kitchen of the light, with Ida in her favorite chair, the old invalid father occupying his corner by the stove, and her mother, with the bright face of Ida's younger sister Hatty, a girl of seventeen, flitting in and out to make up and complete, with the occasional presence of a sailor brother, the family. . . .
>
> And then when our work for the day was done Ida would man her ordinary boat, not the new *Rescue* presented to her by the people of Newport, with its

elaboration of paint, carpet, and gilding, but the familiar old friend in which she won her fame, like herself at once plain, common-sense and reliable. Then with the ready hand of the practiced rower she would play her oars till we were safely landed at the bridge, when waving her farewell with a promise to "tell us more next time we came," she would retrace her billowy way, cleaving the waves with steady stroke, while the ribbons of her sailor hat flutter gaily in the breeze.

Tales of Ida Lewis's skill and courage spread so widely that both President Ulysses S. Grant (1867-1877) and Vice President Schuyler Colfax (cousin of Harriet Colfax, keeper of the Michigan City light—subject of a previous chapter) went to visit her in 1869. Colfax went out to the lighthouse to meet her, but there are two versions of Ida's meeting with President Grant. One says that as Grant landed on Lime Rock, he stepped into water and got his feet wet. "I have come to see Ida Lewis," he remarked, "and to see her I'd get wet up to my armpits if necessary." The other version states that Ida rowed to shore and was conducted to the President's carriage to meet him and his wife.

Ida Lewis in the boat she rowed between the Lime Rock Light and Newport, Rhode Island, and which she used to rescue several people in danger of drowning. Courtesy of the Newport Historical Society.

Fame brought countless other visitors to the island to stare at Ida. Her wheelchair-bound father entertained himself by counting their numbers—often a hundred a day; nine thousand in one summer alone. No wonder Ida helped Brewerton with his pamphlet, for it would relieve her of answering the endless repetitive questions. She also permitted him to paint her portrait and sell photographs of it for 50 cents apiece "throughout the Union." Ida also received numerous gifts, letters, and even proposals of marriage (some of them offering to supply references as to good character). Ida was distressed by all the attention and fended off her many unknown admirers as best she could. Although few details are known, she did marry a Captain William Wilson of Black Rock, Connecticut, in 1870, but they separated after two years.

In 1881 the *Annual Report of the U.S. Life Saving Service* reported that the highest medal awarded by the Life Saving Service had been presented to Mrs. Ida Lewis-Wilson,

> who, under her maiden name of Ida Lewis, has won a national celebrity by her early rescues. The papers accompanying the application made in her case to the Department show that she has saved from drowning thirteen persons, and it is understood that the number is greater. The special instance upon which the medal was awarded, was her rescue, on February 4th [1881], of two soldiers belonging to the garrison of Fort Adams, near Newport, Rhode Island. These men were crossing on foot, at 5 o'clock in the afternoon, or near twilight, between the fort and Lime Rock light-house, of which Mrs. Lewis-Wilson is the keeper, and suddenly fell through the ice, which had become weak and rotten. Hearing their drowning cries, Mrs. Lewis-Wilson ran toward them from the light-house with a rope, and, in imminent danger of the soft and brittle ice giving way beneath her, and also of being dragged into the hole by the men, both of whom had hold of the line she had flung them, she succeeded in hauling first one, and then the other, out of the water. The first man she got out entirely unaided; her brother arrived and helped her with the second. The action on her part showed unquestionable nerve, presence of mind, and dashing courage. The ice was in a very dangerous condition, and only a short time afterward, two [other] men fell through and were drowned, while crossing in the night in the immediate neighborhood of the scene of the rescue. All the witnesses unite in saying that the rescue

Ida Lewis, keeper of Lime Rock Light at Newport, Rhode Island, from 1879 to 1911. Courtesy of the National Archives, #26-LG-69-60.

was accomplished at the imminent risk of the rescuer's life.

Ida's last recorded rescue occurred when she was 63 years old. A close friend, rowing out to the lighthouse, stood up in her boat, lost her balance and fell overboard. Ida, with all the vigor of her past youth, launched a lifeboat and hauled the woman aboard. When asked where she found her strength and courage, she replied, "I don't know, I ain't particularly strong. The Lord Almighty gives it to me when I need it, that's all."[32]

In 1924 the Rhode Island legislature officially changed the name of Lime Rock to Ida Lewis Rock. The lighthouse service changed the name of the Lime Rock Lighthouse to the Ida Lewis Lighthouse—the only such honor ever paid to a keeper. In 1927 the Bureau of Lighthouses removed the lens from the lantern and placed an automated beacon on a skeleton tower in front of the lighthouse. This light continued in service until 1963, when it was deactivated by the Coast Guard. Later the Newport Yacht Club bought the lighthouse and obtained permission from the Coast Guard to put a light back in the old lantern and maintain it as a private aid to navigation. Although adaptively used by the yacht club (and renamed the Ida Lewis Yacht Club), the building is virtually unaltered from the time that Ida Lewis lived there.

Ida Lewis's daring 1869 rescue is immortalized in this painting commissioned by the U.S. Coast Guard. Courtesy of the National Archives, #26-BI-4.

XV. Elizabeth Williams at Beaver Island Harbor Point Light, Michigan, 1872-1884, and Little Traverse Light, Michigan, 1884-1913

Elizabeth Whitney, born on Mackinac Island, Michigan, in 1842, grew up on Beaver Island in Little Traverse Bay. In 1869, some years after she married Clement Van Riper, he was appointed keeper of the Harbor Point Light on the northeast side of the tip of Beaver Island in Lake Michigan. Elizabeth was unusual in the ranks of women keepers in that she nourished many of her solitary hours by writing. Much of her book, *A Child of the Sea; and Life among the Mormons,* deals with her childhood spent near a Mormon settlement on Beaver Island, but the last 20 pages detail her life in two lighthouses on Lake Michigan.

In the spring of 1870 a large force of men came with material to build a new tower and repair the dwelling, adding a new brick kitchen. A new fourth order lens was placed in the new tower and the color of the light changed from white to red. These improvements were a great addition to the station from what it had been. My husband having now very poor health, I took charge of the care of the lamps, and the beautiful lens in the tower was my especial care. On stormy nights I watched the light that no accident might happen. We burned the lard oil, which needed great care, especially in cold weather, when the oil would congeal and fail to flow fast enough to the wicks. In long nights the lamps had to be trimmed twice each night, and sometimes oftener.[33]

Then in 1872 tragedy struck.

One dark and stormy night we heard the flapping of sails and saw the lights flashing in the darkness. The ship was in distress. After a hard struggle she reached the harbor and was leaking so badly she sank. My husband in his efforts to assist them lost his life. He was

Elizabeth Williams kept two lights on Lake Michigan.
Courtesy of Beaver Island Historical Society.

drowned with a companion, the first mate of the schooner *Thomas Howland*. The bodies were never recovered.

Life then seemed darker than the midnight storm that raged for three days upon the deep dark waters. I was weak from sorrow, but realized that though the life that was dearest to me had gone, yet there were others out in the dark and treacherous waters who needed the rays from the shining light of my tower. Nothing could rouse me but that thought, then all my life and energy was given to the work which now seemed was given me to do.

The light-house was the only home I had and I was glad and willing to do my best in the service. My appointment came in a few weeks after, and since that time I have tried faithfully to perform my duty as a light keeper. At first I felt almost afraid to assume so great a responsibility, knowing it all required watchful care and strength, and many sleepless nights. I now felt a deeper interest in our sailors' lives than ever before, and I longed to do something for humanity's sake, as well as earn my living, having an aged mother dependent upon me for a home.[34]

Although her first husband, two brothers, and three nephews died at sea, Elizabeth's own words make it clear that she loved her work.

> From the first, the work had a fascination for me. I loved the water, having always been near it, and I loved to stand in the tower and watch the great rolling waves chasing and tumbling in upon the shore. It was hard to tell when it was loveliest. Whether in its quiet moods or in a raging foam.

> My three brothers were then sailing, and how glad I felt that their eyes might watch the bright rays of our light, shining out over the waste of waters on a dark

Beaver Island Harbor Point Light at the north end of Lake Michigan, kept by Elizabeth Whitney Williams from 1872 to 1884. Only the tower currently remains standing. Courtesy of the National Archives, #26-LG-55-7A.

stormy night. Many nights when a gale came on we could hear the flapping of sails and the captain shouting orders as the vessels passed our point into the harbor, seeking shelter from the storm. Sometimes we could count fifty and sixty vessels anchored in our harbor, reaching quite a distance outside the point, as there was not room for so many inside.[35]

Elizabeth kept the Beaver Island Harbor Point Light for 12 years, staying on even after her second marriage in 1875 to Daniel Williams. In 1884 she requested a transfer to the new lighthouse on Little Traverse Bay, where she remained for 29 years and wrote her book. She gave few details of her career at Little Traverse Light, but the annual reports of the Lighthouse Board report that in 1887, a 45-foot well was sunk to provide fresh water, replaced in 1891 with connections to the city water mains for protection against fire. A fog signal was added in 1896, and a beacon on the breakwater in 1899.[36]

Little Traverse Light at the north end of Lake Michigan was kept by Elizabeth Whitney Williams from 1884 to 1913. The station was deactivated in 1963 and now serves as a private residence. Courtesy of Beaver Island Historical Society.

9. ANNIE BELL HOBBS AT BOON ISLAND LIGHT, MAINE, 1876

Annie Bell Hobbs's father was keeper of the light on Boon Island, off the coast at Kittery, Maine. A lighthouse was first built on this low, flat island during the War of 1812. A new tower of granite, shaped conically, 123 feet high (the tallest such structure along the Maine coast), was constructed in 1855. The lantern was reached by a circular stairway inside the tower. Nearby was the keeper's house and a small frame shed for the lifeboat. A walkway led from a boat slip to the house.

Life on Boon Island was precarious, because the waves washed across the entire island during storms, forcing the keepers to take refuge in the tower. Inclement weather often made it impossible for supply ships to come alongside and tie up. When Annie Bell was about 14 years old, she described life on Boon Island in a short piece published in *Nursery*, a children's magazine of the time. Her simple prose conveys the isolation and loneliness she felt.

Boon Island, Me.,
Jan. 1876

Out at sea, on a rock eight miles from the nearest point of land, and about nine miles east of the town of Kittery, is Boon Island, upon which I have been a prisoner, with the privilege of the yard, the past two years. . . .

I will give you a description of the place and its inhabitants. The island is made up of nothing but rocks, without one foot of ground for trees, shrubs, or grass. The broad Atlantic lies before and all around us. Now and then sails dot the wide expanse, reminding me that there is a world besides the little one I dwell in, all surrounded by water.

The inhabitants of this island consist of eight persons----just the number that entered the ark at the time of the flood. There are three men, the three keepers of the light, whose duties are to watch the light all night, to warn the sailors of danger. There are two families of us, and in my father's family are five members. There are but three children

9. ANNIE BELL HOBBS cont.

in all----my little brother Stephen Green, three years old; little Mamie White of the other family, a little girl of four years, and myself, Annie Bell Hobbs.

Our colony is so small, and the children so few, that the inhabitants have concluded not to build a schoolhouse. Consequently I have my father and mother for teachers. . . .

After school-hours, I turn my eyes and thoughts toward the mainland and think how I should like to be there, and enjoy some of those delightful sleigh-rides which I am deprived of while shut out here from the world.

In the summer we have quite a number of visitors, who board at the beaches during the season. They come to see the lighthouse and all it contains; and we are very glad to show them all, though it is quite tiresome to go up into the light a number of times during the day, since it is one hundred and twenty-three feet from the rock on which it stands to the light.

Up there among the clouds, my father and the other keepers have to watch, night after night, through storms as well as pleasant weather, through summer and winter, the year round, from sunset to sunrise; so that the poor sailors may be warned off from danger.

Annie Bell Hobbs

Not long after Annie Bell sent her account to *Nursery*, the lighthouse service decided that Boon Island was too dangerous for wives and children. Fierce storms often made it impossible for the keepers to get to the mainland or for sailing vessels to bring supplies to Boon Island. The Boon Island lighthouse crew was thereafter restricted to men.[37]

Boon Island Light off the coast of Maine, erected in 1855. Annie Bell Hobbs lived there in 1876 when her father was keeper. Courtesy the U.S. Coast Guard.

10. OTHER 19TH-CENTURY WOMEN KEEPERS

A number of other intrepid women who kept lighthouses for periods exceeding a decade in the second half of the 19th century deserve their tribute. Their names appear in "Lighthouse Keepers and Assistants," but little other information about them has survived:

Angeline Nickerson kept Chatham Light on Cape Cod in Massachusetts from 1848 to 1859.

Mrs. Nuthall (first name unknown) kept Piney Point Light in Maryland from 1850 to 1861. She was not the only woman keeper at Piney Point. Mrs. Elizabeth A. Wilson served there from 1873 to 1877, followed by Mrs. Helen C. Tune for an unknown length of time.

Betsy G. Humphrey took over the light on Monhegan Island in Maine in 1862 when her husband died. At the time she had 10 living children, one son having been killed in the Civil War and one daughter having died in 1854. The surviving children were 23, 21, 20, 19, 13, 10, 9, 6, 4, and 2 years old----several of them obviously old enough to be of considerable help to her. They would also have been company on Monhegan Island, which is some miles off the coast of Maine. Mrs. Humphrey remained at her post until her death in 1880.[38]

Mrs. Julia Toby Brawn was an invaluable aide to her crippled husband in tending the Bay City Light at the mouth of the Saginaw River in Michigan. They moved to the lighthouse, which was funded in those days by subscription from shipowners, in 1862. Peter Brawn died in 1873, and his wife tended the light until 1890, when her son became official keeper.[39]

Mrs. Josephine Freeman succeeded her father as keeper at Blackistone (Black Stone) Island Light, Maryland, in 1876 and tended the light until her death in 1912.[40]

Mary J. Herwerth succeeded her husband at Bluff Point Light on Lake Champlain, New York, in 1881. Like Emma Tabberrah, whom you will meet in Chapter 21, Mary's husband was a disabled Civil War veteran whom she assisted with his keeper's duties until his death. The *Plattsburgh Republican* noted her appointment: "The widow of the late Major Herwerth, light house keeper on Valcour Island, has recently been appointed to the same office. This is as it should be. Mrs. Herwerth was in charge of the light for a long time previous to her husband's death, and the work connected with the office will be just as faithfully done as ever, and this has for years been considered one of the best kept light houses on the lake." Mary apparently continued her duties until 1902.[41]

Bluff Point Light on Lake Champlain, New York, was kept by Mary Herwerth from 1881 to 1902. The light was deactivated in 1930. Courtesy of the National Archives, #26-LG-11-20.

At Squaw Point in Little Bay de Noc on the Upper Peninsula of Michigan, Kate Marvin tended the light from 1897 until 1904. Her husband had also been a disabled Civil War veteran, whose failing health forced him to give up his Baptist ministry. An influential friend in Washington arranged his appointment as keeper of the newly built Squaw Point Light, but he died of pneumonia six months later. Kate, mother of 10 children, still had four at home and was very glad to receive his appointment. Although her closest neighbors lived six miles away and it was a 20-minute row across the bay to Gladstone, the nearest town, Kate was apparently not troubled by the isolation. Books, music, and an occasional trip across the bay were her entertainment.[42]

Point Fermin Light Station in San Pedro, California, was kept by Mary and Helen Smith from 1874 to 1882 and by Thelma Austin from 1925 to 1941. Courtesy of the U.S. Coast Guard.

Mary Smith, Helen Smith, and Thelma Austin

XVI. Mary and Helen Smith, 1874-1882, and Thelma Austin, 1925-1941, at Point Fermin Light, California

Increased shipping into San Pedro Harbor led to the construction of a redwood and fir Victorian lighthouse on Point Fermin at the harbor entrance in 1874. The building design—Italianate with a square tower rising up through the keeper's dwelling—was identical to that of several other lighthouses erected in California at that time. Two large cisterns and the necessary outbuildings were included, with the entire station enclosed by a substantial fence. The lantern panes and the fourth-order Fresnel lens were shipped from France by way of Cape Horn. Lard oil was the first fuel, then kerosene, followed by electricity in 1925.

The first keepers were sisters, Mary and Helen Smith, although only Mary is named as official keeper in 1874 in "Lighthouse Keepers and Assistants." They supposedly took the job in the hope that the exercise would improve their health. Eight years later they decided that life on Point Fermin was too lonely for them. (San Pedro had not yet grown to surround their cliffside dwelling.)

The last keeper at Point Fermin was also a woman. Thelma Austin had gone to Point Fermin in 1917 with her family, when her father was appointed keeper. When both parents died in 1925, Thelma, the eldest daughter, took charge of both the lighthouse and her brothers and sisters. Electrification of the light that year eliminated the endless routine of cleaning, polishing, and lighting lamps every evening and extinguishing them every morning. Thelma's duties were reduced to the flicking of a switch, permitting her to supplement her keeper's salary by working as a dental assistant in the daytime.

Thelma operated the light until two days before Pearl Harbor, when it was "blacked out." During World War II the lantern room was removed and replaced by a radar lookout. An automated light was established nearby after the war, leading the Coast Guard to turn the building over to a private preservation group. It has been restored to its earlier appearance and is today the popular centerpiece of a city park.[43]

Point Fermin on the rugged California coast in 1893. Courtesy of the U.S. Coast Guard.

　　　　　　　　Mary Smith, Helen Smith, and Thelma Austin

11. A FAMILY AFFAIR

Mary and Helen Smith at Point Fermin Light (Chapter 16), Harriet Colfax at Michigan City Light (Chapter 9), and Kate McDougal at Mare Island Light (Chapter 17) were unusual in that they had no prior connection to lighthouses when they were appointed keepers. They differed from the typical women keepers as well in being well-educated and having influential sponsors to help them win their appointments.

As indicated earlier, most of the women who were appointed to tend the lights already were acquainted with lighthouse routines, having learned their arduous duties by helping a father or husband with his work. *Instructions to Light-Keepers*[44] stated specifically, "A light-house must never be left wholly unattended. Where there is a keeper and one or more assistants, either the keeper or one of the assistants must be present. If there is only one keeper, some competent member of his family, or other responsible person, must be at the station in his absence." Teen-age children as well wives shared all the responsibilities for tending the light, often performing heroic acts in their father's or husband's absence. Families carried on the keeper's duties when he could no longer perform them. The lighthouse service benefitted from all this extra unpaid labor.

At the Concord Point Lighthouse in Havre de Grace, Maryland, a single family tended the light for almost a century----from 1829 when the lighthouse was completed until the light was automated in 1920. The first keeper was a hero of the War of 1812 who had valiantly manned the last artillery battery opposing the British at Havre de Grace. The third keeper, Esther O'Neill (1863-78), was the wife of the first keeper's son[45], and followed her husband as keeper. The fourth keeper was her son Henry, followed by his son Henry.

There are also numerous instances of members of lighthouse families marrying into other lighthouse families. Abbie Burgess (Chapter 5), is only one example of a female keeper who married the son of the new keeper after her father was replaced at Matinicus Rock. Fannie Salter, keeper at Turkey Point Light in Maryland (Chapter 22), was related by marriage to the Brumfield and Crouch families, which had provided earlier keepers at that light. Fannie's daughter married back into the Crouch family.

U. S. LIGHT-HOUSE ESTABLISHMENT.
1872.

LIGHT-HOUSE AT MARE ISLAND, CALIFORNIA.

Architect's 1872 rendering of the Mare Island Lighthouse in San Pablo Bay north of San Francisco, from the Report of the Lighthouse Board 1867-1874, *p. 85. Courtesy of the U.S. Coast Guard.*

XVII. Kate McDougal at Mare Island Light, California, 1881-1916

Kate Coffee was born in 1842 in Florence, Alabama, daughter of a U.S. Army officer from an old Southern family.[46] She grew up in New Orleans. Her father's assignments took the family eventually to San Francisco, where Kate demonstrated her independence at an early age by marrying a northern naval officer, Charles J. McDougal, in the year following the end of the Civil War. The northern and southern in-laws always regarded each other somewhat warily.

Shortly after the birth of their first child, Captain McDougal and his sailing vessel *Jamestown* were ordered to carry to Alaska the papers authorizing the purchase of Alaska from Russia (1867). Kate didn't hesitate to accompany him, taking her baby daughter (also named Kate) to spend a year in Sitka.

Then Captain McDougal's ship was ordered around the Horn to Washington, so Kate and her toddler got on the train in San Francisco and crossed the country by rail, two months before the transcontinental railroad was completed (1869). (Presumably stage coaches carried passengers across the gap.) Her second daughter Elizabeth was born shortly after her arrival in Washington.

Her third child Caroline was born after they returned to Oakland. Captain McDougal was then ordered to the "China Station" in Japan. Kate took her three children across the Pacific on a paddle-wheel sailing vessel and spent a year in Yokohama. Her fourth child, Douglas, was born after her return to San Francisco.

Some time in the 1870s Commander McDougal was appointed Inspector of the 12th Lighthouse District, which included the California Coast. Among his duties was the inspection of lighthouses, the delivery of supplies from the lighthouse tender, and the paying of the keepers. In 1881 the lighthouse tender dinghy foundered as he and six others were landing through the heavy surf at the lighthouse at Cape Mendocino. Commander McDougal attempted to swim to shore, but currents carried him away and the heavy money belt he wore around his waist dragged him under the waves. Kate was widowed, with four children between the ages of 8 and 14 and a pension of $50 a month.

Although the Navy did not provide much money for widows in those days, it did try to take care of its own. Charles McDougal's father had been commandant of the Mare Island Naval Shipyard, and relatives were still living there. Charles's Naval Academy classmate George Dewey (of later Spanish-American War fame) arranged for Kate's appointment as keeper of the lighthouse on Mare Island.

The Naval Shipyard sits at the north end of the island and was, after its establishment, connected to San Francisco by a ferry. When the ferry ran aground, the pleas of the naval officers at the shipyard for better aids to navigation were heeded, and the Mare Island Light was constructed in 1873 near the point where the Napa River enters Carquinez Strait and flows into San Pablo Bay.

Photos of the Mare Island Lighthouse from this period show a two-story wooden building of the Italianate style used in several other California lighthouses, with the lantern housed in a square wooden tower. The building was perched on a high cliff, with a long flight of stairs down to the pier. Lighthouse tenders came to this pier every three or four months to leave supplies—oil for the light, food, and in the early days, fresh water. (A rain catch basin for a water system was not constructed until 1890—some years after Kate McDougal took up her post. In 1898 the lighthouse station was connected to the Naval Shipyard water supply.) Supplies were winched up the cliff in a wheeled cart on the rails located to the left of the stairs. A bathroom was installed in the house in 1892.

At the end of the pier was the fogbell, which the keeper activated whenever fog crept across the bay—a frequent and dangerous hazard to shipping. Beside the pier was a beach where Kate's children and grandchildren paddled about in the briny tidal water.

Because of their isolation, family members provided their own social life. Relatives from the Bay area came occasionally to make extended visits. Trips could be made by horse and

Kate McDougal, keeper of the Mare Island Light in California from 1881 to 1916, as a young woman. Courtesy of her granddaughter, Caroline Curtin.

buggy to the Naval Shipyard, but this took time and required some effort. Nor could the light ever be left unattended. It had to be lit every night of the year, and a constant watch kept day and night for approaching fog.

There was no school on the island, nor was it possible to travel daily from the lighthouse to the mainland. Kate McDougal educated her own children as best she could. Her third daughter Caroline did spend a year at a boarding school in San Francisco, but did not continue there. Few girls were educated to go on to college in the 1880s, but Kate's instruction was adequate to prepare her son for the Naval Academy, with some extra tutoring in math.

Kate's granddaughter remembers the base of the lantern tower in the Mare Island Lighthouse being lined with shelves of books, many of them gifts from friends and relatives who realized that Kate and the children needed reading material. All the Oz books were there, the Little Colonel series, and many sets of classics.

United States Navy Yard,
Mare Island, Cal. Jany 21. 1882.

Mrs Kate C. McDougal:—
    My dear Madame—
        Some two months ago many of your friends thought it would be pleasant to be able to wish you a "Merry Christmas" through a telephone, and to have you in closer communication with the inhabited centre of the yard from that time on. So a christmas present of the telephone and its necessary outfit was determined upon.
        Yesterday the work was completed, — a little late perhaps for christmas messages of 1881, but in good time for the many "Merry Christmas's" yet to come that we so heartily wish you.
        In begging you to accept this token of our friendly and sincere appreciation, I am but acting as the mouth piece of those whose

Kate and her eldest daughter loved flowers and planted a beautiful rose garden in front of the lighthouse. They probably also grew their own vegetables. Kate employed a laborer to do the heavy maintenance work, move the oil cart, and care for the cows. Someone constructed a two-room playhouse in the yard for the children, complete with glass windows, wooden floor, and even some cast-off furniture.

The officers at the Naval Shipyard who had known her husband kept track of Kate and assisted her when they could. During her first year on duty, these men put up poles and ran a

1882 letter from the officers of Mare Island Naval Shipyard to Kate McDougal at Mare Island Light Station. Courtesy of her granddaughter, Caroline Curtin.

telephone line from the shipyard to the lighthouse as a Christmas gift for her.

Kate was not a particularly enthusiastic housekeeper, much preferring her duties as light keeper to cooking and cleaning. A Chinese-American cook prepared most of the meals. Occasionally the wife of one of the ranks at the shipyard came to do housework, leaving Kate free to clean the lamps and chimneys, trim the wicks, fill the oil reservoirs, polish the brass and the lenses, and check the mechanisms that revolved around the lamp and rang the fogbell. Every night she opened the curtains in the lantern and lit the light. The last person who went to bed (whether mother, daughter, or granddaughter) was responsible for climbing into the tower to place a fresh lamp inside the lens.

Kate also wrote weekly, monthly, and annual reports, and spent a great deal of time making and recycling clothes for the children. Only the eldest daughter had new dresses. When she outgrew them, they were carefully taken apart, all pieces of material brushed clean and reversed, then reassembled for the next sister. Sometimes, if the material was still not too worn after use by three sisters, pants or jackets were made for brother Douglas.

Because no doctors or dentists were within easy reach, Kate patched and nursed her children as best she could. When her son decided to experiment with the effect of fire on dynamite, a piece of his ear was blown off. Kate retrieved the torn flesh and sewed it back on with a needle and black thread.

Nor was there any church to attend. Daughter Caroline felt this lack, and as a young woman joined a group under the supervision of the chaplain at the Naval Shipyard in planning and raising funds to construct a chapel there.

Kate's eldest daughter married a naval officer. While he was away during the Spanish-American War, his wife and daughter returned to Mare Island to live in the lighthouse. The son-in-law stayed with them between assignments. This arrangement continued until Kate's retirement in 1916, so that one of her granddaughters grew up in Kate's lighthouse. Her son-in-law supplemented the education Kate and her daughter provided, based on his years of teaching English at the Naval Academy.

Kate's second daughter Bessie distinguished herself in 1892 during an explosion at the shipyard. She was passing the naval hospital in her pony cart at the moment of the explosion. She promptly picked up the doctor who came dashing out and drove him to the magazine, where shells were still exploding. A watchman—half-dazed by a blow from a fragment and blinded with blood from a head wound—was stumbling from building to building, closing iron doors and shutters to prevent further disaster. Bessie stopped calmly to tie a bandage around his head, then gave assistance to other wounded until help came and she was ordered out of danger. Her bravery was recognized in an official tribute by the Secretary of the Navy.

After her two older sisters married, Kate's third daughter assumed many of the domestic duties in the household. Young Caroline learned at an early age to clean, do laundry, cook on the wood stove, care for and milk the cow, churn butter, groom the horse, and drive the buggy to the ferry to make trips to town for necessities.

The Mare Island Light Station around the turn of the century. The station no longer exists. Courtesy of Caroline Curtin.

In 1910 a new light (Carquinez Strait Lighthouse) was established across the mouth of the Napa River, eliminating the need for the Mare Island Light. It was abandoned in 1917, only nine days before the Navy Yard's ammunition depot exploded a second time, wrecking 13 buildings. The lighthouse survived, but was razed some time after 1930.

Kate retired in 1916 when an automatic fog signal was installed. All three of her daughters had married military men. Her son, in the Marine Corps, rose to the rank of Brigadier General. Her third daughter, Caroline, married to the medical officer at the Mare Island Naval Shipyard, was living with her family at that time at the other end of the island. Kate went to live with them until her death in 1931.[47]

Kate McDougal after her retirement as keeper of the Mare Island Light in 1916. Courtesy of her granddaughter Caroline Curtin.

XVIII. Laura Hecox at Santa Cruz Light, California, 1883-1917

Laura Hecox was born in 1854 in Santa Cruz, where her father owned two pieces of land. At an early age she tagged after her father, exploring the tidal pools and sandy beaches along the northern edge of Monterey Bay, gathering shells and samples of rocks, minerals, and fossils. She was delighted when her father became keeper of the new Santa Cruz Lighthouse in 1869, permitting her to live on the very shore of her beloved bay. Some of Adna Hecox's ten children were already grown, but he taught the younger ones (Laura was the ninth) to help him in tending the light.

Had Laura been born a hundred years later, she would have gone to college and become a marine biologist. Instead, by the time she reached her twenties, Laura was an amateur student of conchology, corresponding with other shell collectors and exchanging specimens. She also increasingly assumed the duties of caring for the light as her father aged and his health failed.

In 1883 Adna Hecox died. Laura was 29. Her brother-in-law, Captain Albert Brown, recommended to federal officials in San Francisco that Laura be appointed keeper because she knew the duties. Within a week the appointment was made with a salary of $750 a year. Laura lived on in the lighthouse for a total of 47 years. Three of her siblings were married there, and three members of the Hecox family died there. In later years one of Laura's brothers came back to live in the lighthouse, as did a sister and her husband. Laura took care of her mother until she died in 1908 at age 92.

The lighthouse was an ideal post for a conscientious young woman whose avocation was collecting natural artifacts. In an 1896 booklet entitled *Beautiful Santa Cruz County*, Phil Francis writes that "The lighthouse is open to the inspection of the public three days in the week, and Miss Hecox not only exhibits to visitors the curious and costly mechanism of the great lamp, but takes pleasure in showing her own fine and interesting collection of marine curiosities. . . ."

The lamps in the Santa Cruz lantern were fueled before 1870 by high-quality lard oil which was filtered from a half-gallon reservoir located up near the wick so that the heat would keep the oil fluid in cool weather. Lard oil was becoming very expensive—57 cents a gallon, compared to 8½ cents per gallon for kerosene. Santa Cruz Light was one of the first to be converted to the new fuel. An oil house to hold the very flammable liquid was not constructed until 1907. The tiny concrete structure (5 feet by 8 feet) was lined with wooden shelves that held 120 five-gallon cans—a year's supply.

The light was focused to a plane 67 feet above mean sea level by a fourth-order Fresnel lens, about one and one-half feet in diameter, with 18 levels of polished flint glass prisms. Laura kept the lamps, the lens, and the lighthouse in pristine

Santa Cruz Light Station at the north end of Monterey Bay in California was kept by Laura Hecox from 1883 to 1917. This station no longer exists. Courtesy of the National Archives, #26-LG-67-40.

Laura Hecox, keeper of the Santa Cruz Light, collecting rock specimens. Courtesy of Santa Cruz Museum of Natural History.

condition. A writer visiting in 1904 described Miss Hecox as "a most pleasant little woman, standing guard at the front door, armed with a big feather duster." A dusty-looking visitor got a brisk whisking before being admitted inside, for Laura Hecox took *Instructions to Light-Keepers*[48] very seriously: "The utmost neatness of buildings and premises is demanded. Bedrooms, as well as other parts of the dwelling, must be neatly kept. Untidiness will be strongly reprehended, and its continuance will subject a keeper to dismissal. The premises must be kept clean and well whitewashed; grounds in order; all the inside painted work of the lanterns well washed, and, when required, retouched with paint. The spare articles embraced in the list of allowances must be kept on hand and examined frequently, and should be kept clean and in order for use."

Since the keeper's dwelling then housed only Laura and her elderly mother, the six-room house had space to devote one entire room to Laura's private museum. She collected historical artifacts as well as biological specimens, and filled scrapbooks with clippings on taxidermy, architecture, literature, archeology, numismatics, philately, astronomy, religion, geology, botany, and California history.[49]

When a new public library was constructed in Santa Cruz in 1902, Laura Hecox was persuaded to donate her entire collection for permanent display. The Hecox Museum opened in 1905, and included exhibit cases devoted to dried starfish, crustaceans, Indian baskets and mortars, Eskimo artifacts, minerals, agates, gems, South Sea island curios, petrified woods, coral, shells, and turtle and tortoise carapaces.

After her mother's death, Laura remained in the small white keeper's house, faithfully tending the light, until her retirement in 1917 when she was 63 years old. Her death followed two years later.

The historical record does not tell us whether Laura Hecox was frustrated by the limits of her education or career opportunities, or tired by the endless daily routines of the lighthouse, or whether a young man ever came to call on her. But her love of nature made her an indefatigable collector. Laura formed a lasting connection with a museum, guaranteeing that we still catch glimpses of her today in the artifacts and photos connected with the hobby that enlivened the 34 years she kept the Santa Cruz Light.

Laura Hecox and her mother on the porch of the Santa Cruz Lighthouse. Courtesy of the Santa Cruz Museum of Natural History.

Robbins Reef Lighthouse on the west side of New York Upper Bay, marking shoal water on the New Jersey side of the main channel to the Manhattan docks. This light was kept by Kate Walker from 1894 to 1919. Courtesy of the U.S. Coast Guard.

XIX. Kate Walker at Robbins Reef Light, New York, 1894-1919

On the west side of the main channel into the inner harbor of New York City, a mile from Staten Island, is a hidden ridge of rocks that once caused numerous shipwrecks and great loss of life. In 1839 a lighthouse was built on Robbins Reef to guide large ships through Ambrose Channel. Because the ledge is submerged, a masonry island within a caisson was constructed on which to build the original tower.

In 1883 the Lighthouse Board replaced the old stone tower with a four-tier conical iron structure. The light in the 56-foot tower probably used kerosene to fuel the lamp inside a fourth-order Fresnel lens. The flashing mechanism consisted of eight large octagonal lenses set in a heavy frame that revolved between the stationary lantern and the outside windows; these lenses were rotated by a slowly descending weight at a rate that made the steady, diffused light flash brightly every six seconds as the focal point of one of the lenses came opposite the viewer. The light could be seen for 12 miles, except on foggy nights, and was one of the first lights the pilot of an incoming vessel saw when he entered Ambrose Channel. It showed him the way up through the Kill van Kull to Newark Bay, or on past the much brighter Statue of Liberty Light to the Port of New York.

The keeper's quarters fitted around the base of the tower like a donut. The kitchen and dining room were on the main floor. Lockers for clothes and closets for china fitted into the sides of the iron cone. Two bedrooms were on the smaller floor above.

The area of rock above water was hardly larger than the lighthouse itself and provided no mooring for boats. The keeper's skiff hung in davits from the platform. Access to the keeper's quarters was by a vertical steel ladder rising out of the water up to the kitchen door.

To assist mariners in identifying lighthouses in the 19th century, towers were painted in a distinctive combination of colors, which were listed in a *Light List* made available to any navigator by the lighthouse service. The Robbins Reef tower was painted white above and brown below—as it still is today.

The first keeper of the light in the iron tower built in 1883 was John Walker. He had been assistant keeper at Sandy Hook Light. There in the boarding house where he ate his meals, he met a German immigrant woman waiting table. He decided to teach her English, married her, took her to Sandy Hook, and taught her to tend the light. John Walker's bride was in many ways typical of the working women who by 1870 made up one-quarter of all wage earners in the United States. They were either young single women or widows with children to support—many of them immigrants or children of immigrants. Seventy percent of them worked as domestic servants. Kate was an immigrant with a fatherless child, who married a working-class man.

When John Walker received the keeper's appointment on Robbins Reef with a $600 annual salary, Kate was appointed his assistant at $350 a year. She told a visitor that her first reaction to the tiny foothold in the channel was to threaten to leave John Walker. "When I first came to Robbins Reef, the sight of water, which ever way I looked, made me lonesome. I refused to unpack my trunks at first, but gradually, a little at a time, I unpacked. After a while they were all unpacked and I stayed on."[50]

In 1886 John Walker was taken by boat from the lighthouse, ill with pneumonia. His last words to his wife were, "Mind the light, Kate." So she stayed and tended the light. When he died, a substitute was sent to permit Kate to attend his funeral, but she was back on the job before the day ended.

Several men were offered Walker's post, but turned it down because Robbins Reef was too lonely. When Kate, then 40 years old, applied for the keeper's appointment, objections were raised because she was only four feet, ten inches tall and weighed barely one hundred pounds. Time proved that she was as good at her job as any man, for she not only kept the light burning, but rescued as many as 50 people by her own count—mostly fishermen whose boats were blown onto the reef by sudden storms. One such newsworthy incident was the wreck of a three-masted schooner which struck the reef and rolled over onto its side. Kate launched her dinghy and took aboard the five crew members, plus a small Scottie dog, whose survival pleased her enormously.

Kate Walker, who kept Robbins Reef Light off Staten Island in New York Harbor from 1894 to 1919. Photo as it appeared in Harper's Weekly, *Volume 53, August 14, 1909. Courtesy of Virginia State Library and Archives.*

A *New York Times* reporter described Kate Walker in 1906:

> Mrs. Walker is a stolid, self-possessed, observant woman of the North German type, with shrewd gray eyes, hair that is still untouched by the tint of time, and a complexion as ruddy as a sea Captain's. She spends as much time on the terrace outside of her house as she does indoors, even when the wind blows and the salt spray compels her to don an oilskin jacket and a sou'wester. Seen from the decks of passing vessels, this terrace looks as though two goats walking side by side would be crowded. As a matter of fact, three persons arm in arm can promenade it very comfortably. In the good old Summer time, when this terrace is sheltered by an awning and dotted with tables and balcony chairs, it is a very inviting place.
>
> Mrs. Walker serves tea there when the bay is smooth enough for her friends to go out in rowboats to see her. In the Winter, when the water is rough and the lighthouse is surrounded with floating ice half the time, Mrs. Walker is virtually a hermit. But in Summer she is as "merry as they make 'em, . . ." She had a sewing machine and a wind-up phonograph, the latter for the benefit of her son and daughter, who get fidgety once in a while for the sound of a human voice.[51]

Once a year a lighthouse tender brought six tons of coal, a few barrels of oil, and a pay envelope to Mrs. Walker. Other than an occasional inspector's visit, she received little official attention unless the fog signal broke down. The *Times* article emphasized the limits of her horizons:

> All that she knows from personal experience of the great land to which she came as a girl immigrant from Germany is comprised within the limits of Staten Island, New York City, and Brooklyn. She says she has never wanted to go West, South, or anywhere else. Hours of solitude have taught her, she says, that she is in pretty good company when she is by herself, and that happiness is being content with simple things. As a wife, mother, and widow, the happiest and saddest days of her peaceful life have been spent within the circular walls of her voluntary prison. She declares that if she were compelled to live anywhere else she would be the most miserable woman on earth, and that no mansion on Millionaires' Row could tempt her to leave of her own free will.[52]

Assisted by her son Jacob, Kate tended the Robbins Reef Light until her retirement in 1919 at age 73. Her only communication with the mainland was by rowboat or through the periodic calls of the lighthouse tender bringing supplies. She trimmed the wicks while the lamps were burning and kept the reflectors clean and bright. In winter she removed frost from

Robbins Reef Light Station, off Staten Island, was automated in 1966. Courtesy of the U.S. Coast Guard.

inside the glass windows, and during snowstorms climbed outside onto the balcony to clear the snow off the windows. The official instructions were: "To prevent the frosting of the plate glass of lanterns, put a small quantity of glycerin on a linen cloth and rub it over the inner surface of the glass. One application when the lamp is lighted and another at midnight will generally be found sufficient to keep the glass clear during the night."[53]

Mrs. Walker resented any implication that, because she was a lighthouse keeper, she had no household duties in common with other women. "This lamp in the tower, it is more difficult to care for than a family of children. It need not be wound more than once in five hours, but I wind it every three hours so as to take no chances. In nineteen years that light has never disappointed sailors who have depended upon it. Every night I watch it until 12 o'clock. Then, if all is well, I go to bed, leaving my assistant [her son Jacob] in charge."

Jacob had come from Germany with his mother. One cannot help wondering if a fatherless child was the motivation for a young girl to make that frightening voyage alone across the Atlantic to an unknown land. Kate and her husband John Walker had a daughter, Mamie, who boarded with a family on the mainland when it was time to go to school.

Jacob also spent much of his time ashore after his marriage. He was his mother's postman, marketman, and general courier. He also helped her land lumber which washed away from railroad yards and shipyards along the shore—harpooning the logs with a rope and tying them to the railing until low tide when they could be set up to dry.

Among other flotsam brought by the tide, Kate Walker hauled in a small box containing the dead body of a half-dressed baby, with its little hands stretched out as though appealing for help. Later in the morning she lowered the rowboat from the davits and took the lifeless body over to the coroner on Staten Island. Its identity was never known.

The tide also brought occasional comedy to Robbins Reef.

> It is a very swift and treacherous tide around there at times, fully as bad as at Hell Gate. A young man who took his sweetheart out in a rowboat from New Brighton one Summer Sunday afternoon did not heed the warning given to him. The tide carried him squarely onto the rocks around the lighthouse. His boat had a hole in her

bow and was almost full of water when he assisted his companion up the iron ladder and let her have her cry out, while he conferred with the keeper. She dried their clothes while they sat out in the sun in decidedly castaway costume. Jake was ashore as night came on. He might not be back before morning. The girl was in despair.

"We shall miss the last train to Fishkill," she exclaimed, "and I shall have to remain in town all night. Oh, what will they think of me?"

"See here," said the young man. "You say the word and we'll get married on Staten Island tonight and send them a telegram explaining all about it."

The girl was at first indignant, then reluctant, but finally consented. But how to get ashore? As luck would have it, one of Mamie's friends rowed out to the lighthouse that evening to pay a call. He entered into the spirit of the thing. The castaways were taken ashore, married by a minister at the close of the evening service, and started off on a happy honeymoon.[54]

When the light was obscured by fog, as it frequently was in winter, Kate went down into the deep basement and started the engine that sent out siren blasts from a foghorn at intervals of three seconds. The siren made so much noise that she and her son didn't even try to sleep. Occasionally the foghorn machinery broke down. Then Mrs. Walker climbed to the top the tower and banged a huge bell. When the men at the lighthouse station on Staten Island heard the bell, they knew they must visit Robbins Reef and make repairs as soon as wind and weather permitted.

In her years at Robbins Reef Kate Walker saw the progression from kerosene lamps to incandescent oil vapor lamps (similar to today's Coleman lantern) to electricity. The Lighthouse Board began experimenting with electric lights around 1900, and converted those lighthouses near power lines as quickly as possible.

The lighthouse historian Edward Rowe Snow, in his book entitled *Famous Lighthouses of America*, tells another story about Kate Walker—of a Christmas evening that turned into one of her most frightening experiences when a gale blew in:

I knew that to the people coming through the Narrows the snow would hide the light. When I started the foghorn, the snow changed to sleet and drove against the windows. Then, above the driving of the sleet and the rattling of the wind, I heard a sound that I had heard but twice in twenty-five years and dreaded hearing.

We kept our rowboat fastened to the outside walls by a chain, and if that chain broke, and the noise indicated that perhaps it had, I would be helpless to leave the tower.

I wrapped myself up well and went outside. The wind nearly whirled me off the landing, while the sleet covered my hair like a hood. I felt my way along the icy walls. As I thought, one of the chains had been forced loose, and just then the loose end hit me in the eye. But I secured the boat and fought my way back toward the door.

The gale blew in my face as I passed the iron ladder, and began to force me off the balcony. I knew that I could never get a foothold on the icy rungs of the ladder should the wind push me from the balcony. Finally I had to sink to my knees, and work my way to the door where I pushed it open, crawled inside, and shut and locked it. I knew my children would not attempt to return that evening, and so I spent Christmas that night alone in the lighthouse.

After her retirement in 1919, Kate lived on Staten Island. She died in 1931 at the age of 83. Her obituary in the *New York Evening Post* contained a moving passage:

A great city's water front is rich in romance. There is a strangeness about the restless ships that know the other side of the world; there are queer men busy in curious occupations; there are mysteries of sky and sea and weather. There are the queenly liners, the grim battle craft, the countless carriers of commerce that pass in endless procession. And amid all this and in sight of the city of towers and the torch of liberty lived this sturdy little woman, proud of her work and content in it, keeping her lamp alight and her windows clean, so that New York Harbor might be safe for ships that pass in the night.

Today, the Robbins Reef light is automated, and the lighthouse is closed to the public.[55]

XX. Margaret Norvell at Port Pontchartrain Light, Louisiana, 1896-1924, and West End Light, Louisiana, 1924-1932

Margaret Norvell carried on her husband Louis's duties as keeper of Head of Passes Light in Louisiana after he drowned in 1891, leaving her with two small children. According to "Lighthouse Keepers and Assistants" in the National Archives, Margaret Norvell was appointed official keeper of the Port Pontchartrain Light on Lake Pontchartrain in Louisiana in 1896.

The lighthouse was located near the east terminus of the Pontchartrain Railroad, where the town of Milneburg was a transshipment point and stop-over for passengers on the way to and from the lake's north shore health resorts. The tower elevated the light 35 feet above sea level, making it visible 10 miles. According to a *Times Picayune* article in 1934, Mrs. Norvell kept chickens and a Spitz dog in her yard, and a talking parrot in her kitchen. Her living room was lined with books and graced by a piano.

An account of Madge Norvell's career in the *Morning Tribune* of 26 June 1932 recounts the many lives she saved. "I have often rung my fogbell," she said, "to get help for overturned boats or to signal directions to yachts." During one storm, she threw a rope to the crews of both a yacht and a schooner, bringing them safely into the lighthouse and providing food and shelter for several days until the storm abated. On other occasions she rescued people from disabled sailboats and a small plane blown into the lake in a squall.

The article goes on: "It is not only the shipwrecked to whom Mrs. Norvell opened her doors. In every big hurricane or storm here since 1891, her lighthouse has been a refuge for fishermen and others whose homes have been swept away. In the . . . storm of 1903 Mrs. Norvell's lighthouse was the only building left standing on the lower coast, and over 200 survivors found a welcome and shelter in her home. After each storm she started the relief funds and helped the poor folk get back to normal."

A surprising career for a woman who came from a socially prominent New Orleans family and married a well-to-do cotton broker. His loss of his fortune led the Norvells into the lighthouse service, and Madge must have learned to love the lights. After her retirement she went every evening at sunset to the seawall to watch for the first flashing of the beacon she had tended. In her own words, "there isn't anything unusual in a woman keeping a light in her window to guide men folks home. I just happen to keep a bigger light than most women because I have got to see that so many men get safely home."[56]

The oil lamps at Port Pontchartrain were discontinued in 1929 and the tower turned over to the Orleans Parish Levee Board. Newspaper accounts of Mrs. Norvell's death in 1934 indicated that she also tended the electrified light in the West End Lighthouse on Lake Pontchartrain from 1924 until 1932.

Port Pontchartrain Light on Lake Pontchartrain in Louisiana, kept by Margaret Norvell from 1896 to 1924. Courtesy of the National Archives, #26-LG-37-51.

XXI. Emma Tabberrah at Cumberland Head Light, New York, 1904-1919

In 1867 Emma Dominy of Beekmantown, New York, married William Tabberrah from a farm near Beekmantown.[57] Because William was a disabled veteran of the Civil War, he was advised to apply for the position of keeper of the light at Cumberland Head on Lake Champlain. He received that appointment in 1871, moving Emma and her two babies into the new limestone block quarters beside the much older conical tower.

In spite of his disability, William kept the light for 33 years. He purchased an 89-acre farm adjoining the lighthouse property, which enabled him to indulge his love of horses. The town of Plattsburgh was seven miles away, requiring horse-and-buggy transportation to reach it.

Six more Tabberrah children were born in the lighthouse. William was continually plagued by a lead bullet lodged in his hip since the Civil War. In 1903, surgery to remove the bullet led to an infection which killed him. Emma applied for his job and was appointed keeper in 1904 at a salary of $480 a year, serving until her retirement in 1919 (when she received a pension of $190.17 per year). Two of her daughters kept her company and assisted her with her keeper's duties.

The tower was 50 feet high, putting the focal beam from the Fresnel lens 75 feet above the lake level and making it visible for 11 miles. An oil room connected the tower to the keeper's house and served to store kerosene and lamps as well as a workbench and tools. The daily cleaning and maintenance of the lamps was done there.

The first floor of the keeper's house had a parlor, a dining-sitting room, and a pantry. The kitchen was in a one-story addition at the back of the house. Upstairs were two large and two small bedrooms, above them an unfinished attic. Wood

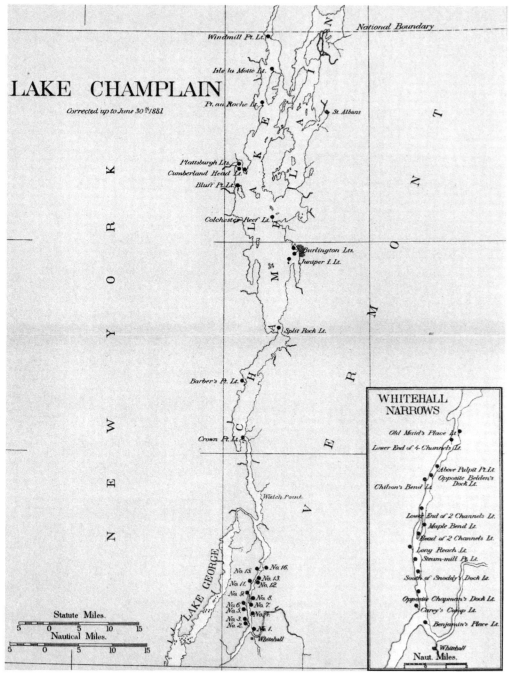

1881 Annual Report of the Lighthouse Board.

stoves in the kitchen and the sitting room heated the house. An outbuilding contained a carriage house, a stable for two horses, a woodshed, and an outhouse. In the 19th century the family did without plumbing, electricity, or a telephone.

Had Emma Tabberrah recorded her memories, she doubtless would have discussed cleaning and polishing the lamps in the oil room, as well as the daily routine of climbing the stairs at sunset to place the lamps in the lantern, replacing them with fresh lamps at midnight, and extinguishing them at sunrise. Then she carried them back to the oil room and polished them again. She would have climbed the stairs frequently to polish the many prisms of the fourth-order Fresnel lens that magnified the light.

But what her children remembered and passed on to their children were the charming details of family life in a rural lighthouse in the late 19th century. Rain water for household washing and bathing was collected in a basement cistern and pumped by hand into the kitchen sink. The well on the property had a heavy concentration of sulphur, giving it a strong taste. Emma was the only one who liked it well enough to drink it. The others brought drinking water in pails from Lake Champlain.

Fortunately the local school was only a mile away so the children could walk, ski, or snowshoe up through the woods behind their home to the main road. As they grew older, three of the girls went to board in Plattsburgh while taking teacher training, and later taught in the area and downstate. As for playmates, there were very few neighbors except for summer residents in the cottages on Lake Champlain. The children were always overjoyed when cousins arrived to spend long summer holidays at the lighthouse.

The family provided its own entertainment. The children were encouraged to learn to identify the habits of woodland animals and birds. They often cared for injured birds. They played croquet on the lawn and tennis on their homemade court. They tended the garden and went on excursions to gather flowers and berries. In the summer they could fish and sail on the lake and take picnics to the beach, and in winter they went ice-boating. The girls learned sewing and embroidery as well as cooking. The boys helped their father operate the farm.

They had a piano and their father played the flute. Sunday afternoons were special because Emma dressed in her best gown and received callers in the parlor. Guests must be offered refreshments, and the children loved nothing better than bringing ice (cut from the lake in the winter and stored in an ice house in the woods) to pack into a hand-cranked ice cream freezer. They took turns working the crank and licking the paddles when it was done.

In 1894 an open-air chapel was constructed in the woods south of the ferry slip. Sunday services were conducted there by ministers of the area, as well as by some summer residents. The building was also used for occasional community picnics or a dramatic presentation by the young people.

In 1904 the Tabberrahs' daughter Rose married Milo Hillegas under the walnut tree on the lighthouse lawn. This happy occasion was followed only three months later by her father's death. He had been bedridden for two years, requiring Emma to be both constant nurse and keeper of the light.

After her 15 years keeping the Cumberland Head Light, Emma retired and spent another 14 years with her daughter Maud in Beekmantown, devoting her days to her children and grandchildren. She was buried beside her husband in Plattsburgh, New York.

In 1934 a skeleton tower was built by the lake shore to hold an automated acetylene light. Since the old lighthouse was no longer needed, it was sold to private owners, who in 1948 began restoration of the keeper's house as a private dwelling. In 1984 the Town of Plattsburgh adopted on its official seal a drawing of the old Cumberland Head Light.

Seal of the Town of Plattsburgh, New York, with the Cumberland Head Light as its focus. Courtesy of the Plattsburgh Town Historian.

Emma Tabberrah, keeper of the Cumberland Head Light on Lake Champlain from 1904 to 1919, after her retirement. Courtesy of her grandson, Arthur B. Hillegas.

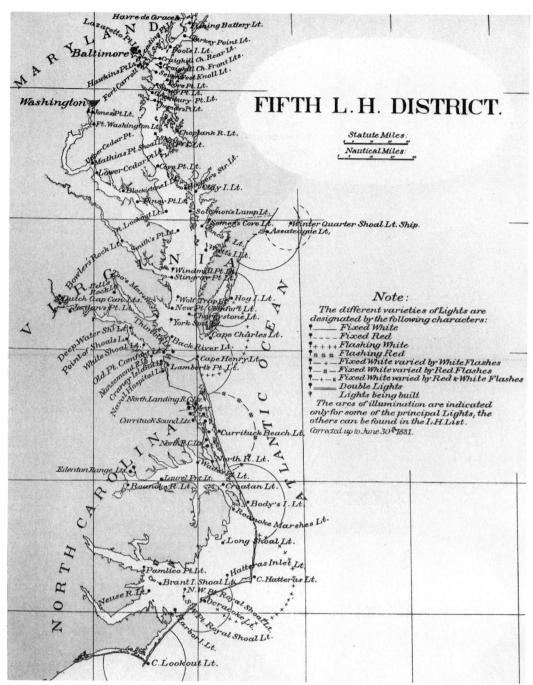

1881 Annual Report of the Lighthouse Board.

XXII. Fannie Salter at Turkey Point Light, Maryland, 1925-1947

The lighthouse at Turkey Point, Maryland, was built of dressed stone in 1833. Only 38 feet tall, its location on a bluff at the southern tip of Elk Neck is 100 feet above the bay, making the light visible for 13 miles.

Turkey Point Light was kept by women longer than any other light on the Chesapeake Bay—and indeed almost as long as Biloxi Light in Mississippi. Elizabeth Lusby kept the light from 1844 to 1861. Rebecca Crouch was appointed keeper after her husband died in 1873, and served until 1895. She was succeeded by her daughter, Georgianna Crouch Brumfield, who remained until 1919.

Fannie Mae Salter was the last civilian woman to keep a light along the 40,580 miles of coastline and river channels in the United States. When her keeper husband died in 1925, Mrs. Salter was told that Civil Service rules would prevent her succeeding him because of her age. She appealed to her senator, who went to the White House and asked President Coolidge to appoint her to the post. She was keeper at Turkey Point from 1925 until 1947.

Mrs. Salter's logs are archived in the Suitland, Maryland, repository of the National Archives. Each day she recorded the weather, and, like Harriet Colfax, she occasionally added personal comments to her logs. Here are a few examples that show the routine of her daily life as she began her career as official keeper:

April 1, 1925: Northwest fresh, cloudy. Received telegram that I have been appointed as permanent keeper of this Station by Pres. Coolidge. Went to North East [a nearby Maryland town] for supplies. Painted in lantern. Cleaned lens to-day.

April 6: Northeast fresh a.m., calm p.m. clear. Cleaned brass to-day.

April 9: Southwest moderate clear. Painted lantern floor & platform below. Unpacking furniture.

April 16: North to northeast fresh clear. Scrubbed lantern, cleaned cellar, pumped water out of boat.

April 20: Northeast fresh, cloudy clearing to west p.m. Keeper left 6:30 a.m. for Balto. on official business. Returned same day 10:15 p.m.

April 23: Southwest rain in early morning, but cleared off pretty. Recharged fire extinguisher.

April 27: South to west light fair. Put screens in windows, shellacked two floors.

Fannie Salter and her son feed turkeys on the lawn of Turkey Point Lighthouse at the head of the Chesapeake Bay. In 1993, only the tower remains. Courtesy of the Ralph Smith Collection, The Mariners' Museum, Newport News, Virginia.

April 29: Northeast fresh cloudy. Pumped water out of boat. Scrubbed lantern floor.

September 2: West to southwest light, partly cloudy. Cleaned storm panes inside and out.

September 4: Light westerly winds partly cloudy. Had bushes cut down round the bank.

September 5: Northwest light, fair. Cleaned tower from top to bottom & bell house.

September 8: Light northwest partly cloudy. Mowed lawn.

September 9: Moderate southwest hazy. Tender Juniper delivered medicine, wheelbarrow & parts for stove.

September 10: Moderate to calm southwest, hazy, hot. Tender Juniper passed this Station this p.m. after relighting aids to navigation up the Susquehanna.

Fannie Salter and her Cheasapeake Bay retriever go about chores at the Turkey Point Lighthouse. Courtesy of the Ralph Smith Collection, The Mariners' Museum, Newport News, Virginia.

September 17: West moderate, clear cool. Finished painting exterior of bell house.

September 18: Moderately southerly winds partly cloudy. Whitewashed interior of toilet, painted the wood.

September 19: West moderate fair. Painted tower floor, handrail and ladder, scrubbed tower steps.

September 21: Tender Maple arrived with wood & coal, also fogbell machinery, and Mr. Lenord came to install same.

September 29: Northwest light, partly cloudy. Painted new woodwork in bell house.

Until 1943, when electricity was installed at Turkey Point, Mrs. Salter found it necessary to make four or five trips daily to the top of the tower. When a 100-watt electric bulb was placed inside the Fresnel prism, increasing the light to 680 candlepower, the keeper's back-breaking duties were reduced to the mere flip of a switch. Then one trip a day up the tower kept the light in working order. Only during cold weather were additional trips necessary to defrost the huge windows surrounding the light. The heavy brass oil lamps used earlier were kept in readiness in case the electric power and auxiliary plant should malfunction (the auxiliary plant was supposed to go into operation automatically when the electric power failed).

Like other lighthouse keepers, Mrs. Salter maintained a radio watch and was on duty seven days a week, 24 hours a day. She was in constant communication with aids-to-navigation authorities and made reports of local weather conditions and other necessary information by a radio telephone set, installed by the Coast Guard during World War II. Although no instruction in its use was provided, Fannie mastered the radio with the aid of the accompanying manual.

Snow-blocked roads often marooned Mrs. Salter many weeks at a time during the winter, leaving radio and telephone as her only means of communication with the outside world. She fed herself from her well-stocked vegetable cellar, where shelves were lined with home-canned jars of vegetables and fruits which she grew on the lighthouse's three-acre plot. Loneliness was relieved by a Chesapeake Bay retriever, a flock of chickens, and a dozen head of lambs and sheep. In the early years of Mrs. Salter's tenure, laundry, bakery, and ice trucks made deliveries to the lighthouse, but World War II put an end to the long trips over the seven-mile road through Elk Neck State Park.

"And when I get tired of things outdoors, I always have my hobby—crossword puzzles, " Mrs. Salter said. "I never seem to get enough of crossword puzzles," she smiled. "My friends send me many hundreds, but I'm always 'fresh out'. Most of my evenings are spent on crossword puzzles and reading."[58]

Fannie Salter had three children, all married except Bradley, the youngest, who helped her with some of the heavier chores about the light station.

Talking over her early days as keeper of the light at Turkey Point, Mrs. Salter recalled one of her most frightening

Fannie Salter's daughter Mabel rings the fog bell at Turkey Point Light Station in the 1930s. Courtesy of the Ralph Smith Collection, The Mariners' Museum, Newport News, Virginia.

experiences. "It was a cold night and very foggy out," she said. "I was alone with my seven-year-old son at the time. Suddenly the whistle of a boat, apparently making for Philadelphia, was heard around our point. I started the bell ringing, but almost immediately a cable connected to the striking mechanism snapped.

"I began to pull the bell, counting to fifteen between each pull. It was necessary to ring the bell four times a minute. I kept this up for about 55 minutes, until the ship was safely around the point and headed for the Chesapeake and Delaware Canal.

Fannie Salter polishes the Fresnel lens in the lantern of Turkey Point Light. Courtesy of the U.S. Coast Guard.

I was never more exhausted in my whole life. It certainly was one experience I never want to relive," she said.

Modern floating aids to navigation did away with the bell's necessity, but Mrs. Salter's duties included checking and reporting on the various buoys, channel lights, and other aids in her area so they were kept in proper position and working order.

When asked about retirement plans in 1945, she said, "I plan to stay as long as the Coast Guard wants me. Perhaps after the war I'll make other plans." She smiled when she added, "Maybe I couldn't sleep away from the light. You see, its bright beam has been shining through my bedroom window for so many years its presence has become my security and companion. Whenever the light goes out I wake up immediately."

When she finally retired in 1947, she moved to a house six miles away, where she could still see her beloved light flashing. Later she lived in Baltimore until her death in 1966 at age 83.[59]

At Turkey Point, the Coast Guard tore down the outbuildings and the keeper's house, also destroying the brick stairway in the tower so that vandals could not reach the light. Trees have grown up around the base, partially obscuring the tower, but the light is still active and the grounds accessible in Elk Neck State Park.

Fresnel lens from the Point Fermin Light in 1912, complete with incandescent oil vapor lamp and clockwork system used to rotate the bulls-eye lens to achieve a flashing effect. Courtesy of the National Archives, #26-LG-65-41A.

XXIII. The U.S. Coast Guard Runs the Lighthouse Service

As the 19th century drew to a close, the lighthouse service was becoming more and more professional. Inexperienced amateurs with political clout no longer received keeper's appointments which they could hold until they died. Instead, young men were encouraged to join the service at the bottom rank, such as seaman on a tender, and work their way up, being promoted and transferred from post to post. In 1896 lighthouse keepers were included in the classified Civil Service and were expected to have specific qualifications.

Many of the lights were being electrified after the turn of the century. Before electric power was available, many lenses were revolved by a large clockwork, propelled by a hand-cranked weight suspended inside the lighthouse tower. This old-fashioned equipment was replaced by electric equipment, as were the kerosene and coal-burning boilers firing steam foghorns, eliminating the need for a keeper on 24-hour-a-day duty. Large towers were often replaced with smaller skeletal structures which didn't require the constant attention and upkeep of earlier stations.

The first experiments with automatic lights were made in the 1920s. The radio beacon was introduced in Coast Guard stations in 1921—a much more sophisticated means of determining location than depending on a landmark such as a lighthouse by day or a light by night. Neither are needed when ships have sophisticated radar equipment that permits a navigator to "see" the shore up to 20 miles away on a screen.

In 1910 Congress replaced the Lighthouse Board with a Bureau of Lighthouses, located within the Commerce Department. By this date the United States had 11,713 aids to navigation (lighthouses, post lights, buoys, lightships, etc.) along its coasts and rivers. The man selected to head the new bureau, George R. Putnam, was determined to eliminate politics from the lighthouse service. District supervisor and inspector posts were transferred from military officers to civilians—generally career lighthouse service employees, thus forging a truly professional organization.[60]

These changes affected the status of women in the lighthouse service. A 1948 *Coast Guard Bulletin* included the following comments about women keepers, implying that modern technology had deprived them of lighthouse service careers:

> In days gone by, the duties and lives of these women keepers were often arduous in the extreme, but principally because of the great isolation of the sites on which many lighthouses were built, and the lack of modern conveniences. These women often performed acts of heroism, not unexpected where they lived so surrounded by the sea; and on numerous occasions made personal sacrifices that the signals under their charge might not fail the mariners.
>
> It was the development of steam for signals and their coal-fired boilers, and the later introduction of heavy duty internal combustion engines, which first placed the duties of keepers of lighthouses beyond the capacity of most women. Their gradual retirement from this field of employment was further hastened when intricate electrical equipment was placed at many stations, and when the duties of lighthouse keepers gradually came to require special training and when many of the newer stations were built offshore on submarine foundations. As these changes took place, those women who remained in the lighthouse service were transferred to or were retained at stations where the equipment was of a more simple type. Soon still other developments and inventions were to invade the field of the woman keeper, for in those quiet backwaters, where comparatively primitive equipment was still found adequate, it was found that automatic apparatus could be effectively substituted, and many smaller lighthouses were converted into automatically operated stations or made parts of groups of lights tended by keepers who maintained a patrol by means of smaller boats. These changes practically closed the lighthouse field to women.

The maintenance of aids to navigation was transformed after 1939 when the lighthouse service was abolished and its duties turned over to the United States Coast Guard. As part of the transition, personnel in the lighthouse service were given the choice of continuing their civilian status or converting to a military rank at no loss of pay. Those who chose to remain civilians gradually reached retirement age and the era of the civilian keeper ended.

The Coast Guard continued the steady improvements in aids to navigation, including the introduction of loran (long-range navigation) and shoran (short-range navigation) by which the navigator determines his ship's position from radio signals received from Coast Guard stations. Coast Guard personnel (both men and women) are systematically trained to perform a vast array of duties, including maintaining aids to navigation, and are periodically rotated from assignment to assignment. Today some 475 automated lights operating along our coasts are maintained by the Coast Guard.

Fog signal equipment used at New Dungeness Light Station in 1908. Courtesy of the National Archives, #26-LG-62-14.

Some lighthouses still use Fresnel lenses and an electric light bulb, all automated, but more powerful aerobeacons with a 1,000-watt lamp are used where needed. The most efficient lights today have a simple plastic lens around a solar-powered lamp, mounted on a platform or pole—a startling contrast to the tall towers that housed the beacons in decades past.

Gradually the isolation of many light stations was relieved by radio, television, libraries, liberal leave, and beach jeeps for driving in rough terrain. Today, with the exception of the light in Boston Harbor (which by special act of Congress in 1989 is to remain permanently manned to preserve its special historic character), the era of manned light stations is over.

Women in the Coast Guard continued to tend the lights. The light at the Dofflemyer Point Lighthouse near Olympia, Washington, was automated (turned on and off by a photoelectric cell) in the 1960s, but not the fog signal. In 1965 Madeline Campbell was appointed keeper of the Dofflemyer Point Lighthouse. Her husband and son helped her maintain the equipment. So important was the fog signal that they would check the weather predictions and get a sitter to operate it if they were to be away from home in foggy weather. Mrs. Campbell kept her post until the fog signal was automated in 1987. Even then, because she lived nearby she kept an eye on the station and informed the Coast Guard if anything needed attention.

In 1980, Jeni Burr, Seaman First Class, was appointed keeper at New Dungeness Lighthouse, located on a seven-mile-long sand spit in the Strait of Juan de Fuca in Washington State. The light had been automated in 1976, but Jeni and her husband, Eric, maintained the grounds and buildings, living in the keeper's house built in 1905 with their five cats and two dogs. At high tide they were cut off from the mainland, so resorted to boat or timed their jeep trips to town by the tides.[61]

In a 1986 issue of *The Keeper's Log* (Volume II, Number 2), Karen McLean was listed as keeper of three lights—the Doubling Point range lights and Squirrel Point—along the Kennebec River in Maine. Her husband Don was in charge of a nearby unit in Boothbay. They lived in a small white frame house between the two stations.

Epilogue

Although the era of the resident lighthouse keeper has ended, our attachment to lighthouses continues. Landmarks are important to orienting us in our terrain, and lighthouse towers serve as daymarks for those on land and water alike, helping to define our sense of place. The destruction of a lighthouse tower leaves a landscape blighted, disturbingly emptied. The symbolism of lighthouses still grips us—their assurance of security for those in peril on the sea, of a lifeline to safety, of guidance to solid footing on the shore.

Much individual effort is devoted to maintaining these reminders of a more romantic past. The Coast Guard tries to find custodians who will preserve the integrity of both automated stations and stations no longer needed as active aids to navigation. Imaginative adaptive uses range from marine research laboratories to bed-and-breakfast inns. Historical societies and local authorities have assumed responsibility for preserving, interpreting, and keeping the lighthouses in their communities intact, often turning them into museums or historic sites that permit hundreds of visitors to explore them. Over 200 American lighthouses are currently accessible to the public; 35 of these are in national parks.[62]

Although in many cases only the grounds of the stations are open to the public, visitors can still climb a number of the towers and see the old Fresnel lens displayed, recreating mental images of the sturdy keeper going about his duties there. If those images summon up stalwart men lighting and watching the lights night after night after night, regardless of monotony or inclement weather, these chapters should serve as a reminder that dozens of intrepid women also climbed those stairs and lit those lamps and polished those lenses. Their dedication to ensuring the safety of the seamen on the ships that plied our coasts and waterways matched that of their male colleagues, and they too should be remembered and honored for their courage and devotion.

Round Island Light in Mississippi Sound in 1893. Margaret Anderson was keeper from 1872 to 1881. The keeper's quarters burned in 1954, but the deactivated tower still stands. Courtesy of the National Archives, #26-LG-37-60.

Appendix: Women Who Kept the Lights

Alabama:

Choctaw Point
Mobile Bay

Carmalite Philibert
1842 - 1852
Replaced: Husband

California:

Angel Island Light
San Francisco Bay

Juliet Nichols
1902 - 1914
Replaced: John Ross

Humboldt Bay Light
Humboldt Bay Entrance

Sarah E. Johnson
1858 - 1863
Replaced: J. Johnson (Husband)

Mare Island Light
San Pablo Bay

Kate C. McDougal
1881 - 1916
Replaced:

Point Fermin Light
San Pedro Harbor

Mary L. Smith
1874 - 1882
Replaced:

Point Fermin Light
San Pedro Harbor

Thelma Austin
1925 - 1941
Replaced: Father

Point Pinos Light
Monterey Bay

Charlotte A. Layton
1856 - 1860
Replaced: Charles Layton (Husband)

Point Pinos Light
Monterey Bay

Emily A. Fish
1893 -1914
Replaced: Alan Luce

Santa Barbara Light
Santa Barbara Channel

Julia F. Williams
1865 - 1905
Replaced: Albert Williams (Husband)

Santa Barbara Light
Santa Barbara Channel

Caroline Morse
1905 - 1911
Replaced: Julia Williams

Santa Cruz Light
North End Monterey Bay

Laura J. Hecox
1883 - 1917
Replaced: Adna Hecox (Father)

Connecticut:

Black Rock (Harbor) Light
Fayerweather Island

Catherine A. Moore
1871 - 1878
Replaced: Stephen Moore (Father)

Bridgeport Breakwater Light
West Side of Harbor Entrance

Flora McNeil
1904 - 1911
Replaced: Stephen McNeil (Husband)

Morgan's Point Light
Mystic River Mouth

Eliza Daboll
1838 - 1854
Replaced: Husband

North Dumpling Light
Fishers Island Sound (New York waters)

Catherine Gunn
1876 -
Replaced: John Gunn (Husband)

Stonington (Harbor) Light
East Side of Harbor

Patty Potter
1842 - 1854
Replaced: Husband

Stratford Point Light
Long Island Sound

Amy Buddington
1853 -
Replaced:

Delaware:

Bombay Hook Light
Delaware River at Smyrna River Mouth

Margaret Stuart
1850 - 1862
Replaced: Duncan Stuart (Father)

Oak Island Light
Delaware River

Maria Allen
1879 -
Replaced: J. Allen (Husband)

Florida

Key West Light
Whiteheads Point

Barbara Mabrity
1832 - 1864
Replaced: Michael Mabrity (Husband)

Key West Light
Whiteheads Point

Mary Bethel
1908 - 1914
Replaced: William Bethel (Husband)

Pensacola Light
Pensacola Bay

Michaela Ingraham
1840 - 1855
Replaced: Jeremiah Ingraham (Husband)

Sand Key Light Florida Keys	Rebecca Flaherty 1830 - 1846 Replaced: John Flaherty (Husband)
St. Johns River Light St. Johns River Entrance	Frances McDonald 1871 - 1879 Replaced: Alexander McDonald (Husband)
St. Marks Light Appalachee Bay/St. Marks River	Ann Dudley 1850 - 1854 Replaced: Needham Dudley (Husband)
St. Marks Light Appalachee Bay/St. Marks River	Sarah J. Fine 1904 - 1909 Replaced: Charles Fine (Husband)

Georgia:

Oyster Beds Beacon Savannah River Channel	Mary Maher 1853 - 1856 Replaced: Cornelius Maher (Husband)
Tybee Beacon Savannah River Entrance	Frances O. Sickel 1870 - Replaced:

Indiana:

Calumet Harbor Light Calumet Harbor, Lake Michigan	Mary Ryan 1873 - 1880 Replaced: Husband
Michigan City Light Lake Michigan	Harriet E. Colfax 1861 - 1904 Replaced: John M. Clarkson

Louisiana:

Bayou St. John Light Lake Pontchartrain East Entrance	Annie Gage 1895 - 1906 Replaced:
Bayou St. John Light Lake Pontchartrain East Entrance	Minnie E. Coteron 1906 - Replaced: Mrs. Annie Gage
New Canal Light Lake Pontchartrain Canal Entrance	Mary F. Campbell 1869 - 1895 Replaced: Augustus Campbell (Husband)
New Canal Light Lake Pontchartrain Canal Entrance	Caroline Riddle 1895 - 1924 Replaced: Mary F. Campbell

New Canal (West End) Light Lake Pontchartrain Canal Entrance	Margaret R. Norvell 1924 - 1932 Replaced: Caroline Riddle
Pass Manchac Light West Shore Lake Pontchartrain	Mary J. Succow 1873 - 1909 Replaced: Anthony Succow (Husband)
Port Pontchartrain Light Lake Pontchartrain	Ellen Wilson 1882 - 1895 Replaced:
Port Pontchartrain Light Lake Pontchartrain	Margaret R. Norvell 1896 - 1924 Replaced: Louis O. Norvell (Husband)
Port Pontchartrain Light Lake Pontchartrain	Mrs. W. E. Coteron 1924 - 1929 Replaced: Margaret R. Norvell
West Rigolets Light Rigolets Channel	Anna M. Read 1898 - Replaced:

Massachusetts:

Annisquam Harbor Light Annisquam Harbor/Ipswich Bay	Mary Phipps 1871 - Replaced: Octavius Phipps
Chatham Light Chatham Harbor/Cape Cod	Angeline M. Nickerson 1848 - 1859 Replaced:
Marblehead Light Marblehead Neck/Massachusetts Bay	Jane E. Martin 1860 - 1863 Replaced:
Mayo's Beach Light Cape Cod	Sarah Atwood 1876 - Replaced: William Atwood (Husband)
Plymouth (Gurnet Point) Light Plymouth Bay	Hannah Thomas 1776 - 1786 Replaced: John Thomas (Husband)
Sandy Neck Light Cape Cod	Lucy J. Baxter 1862 - 1867 Replaced: F. T. D. Baxter (Husband)

Maryland:

Blackistone Island Light St. Clements Island/Potomac River	Josephine Freeman 1876 - 1912 Replaced: Joseph L. McWilliams (Father)

Cove Point Light Patuxent River Entrance/Chesapeake Bay	Sarah Thomas 1857 - 1859 Replaced:
Fishing Battery Island Light Upper Chesapeake Bay	Sarah Levy 1853 - 1855 Replaced:
Fort Carroll Light West of Sparrows Point/Chesapeake Bay	Sarah E. Meeds 1901 - Replaced: James Meeds (Husband)
Havre de Grace (Concord Pt.) Light Upper Chesapeake Bay/Susquehanna River	Esther O'Neill 1867 - 1878 Replaced: John O'Neill (Husband or Brother)
Hawkins Point Light Chesapeake Bay	Helen I. Waterworth 1871 - Replaced:
North Point (Two Lights)	Elizabeth Riley 1834 - 1857 Replaced:
North Point Light	H. Schmuck 1864 - 1866 Replaced: Henry Schmuck (Husband)
Piney Point Light Potomac River	Nuthall 1850 - 1861 Replaced:
Piney Point Light Potomac River	Elizabeth C. Wilson 1873 - 1877 Replaced:
Piney Point Light Potomac River	Helen C. Tune 1877 - Replaced:
Point Lookout Light Potomac River Entrance	Martha A. Edwards 1853 - 1855 Replaced:
Point Lookout Light Potomac River Entrance	Pamela Edwards 1855 - 1869 Replaced: Martha Edwards (Mother)

Point Lookout Light	Ann Davis
Potomac River Entrance	1830 - 1847
	Replaced: James Davis (Husband)

Sandy Point Light	Mary E. Jewell (Yewell?)
Upper Chesapeake Bay	1860 - 1861
	Replaced: William Jewell (Yewell?) (Husband)

Sharp's Island Light	Harriet Valliant
Chesapeake Bay	1851 - 1856
	Replaced:

Turkey Point Light	Elizabeth Lusby
Elk River Entrance/Chesapeake Bay	1844 - 1861
	Replaced: Robert Lusby (Husband)

Turkey Point Light	Rebecca L. Crouch
Elk River Entrance/Chesapeake Bay	1873 - 1895
	Replaced: John Crouch (Husband)

Turkey Point Light	Georgiana C. Brumfield
Elk Neck River/Chesapeake Bay	1895 - 1919
	Replaced: Rebecca Crouch (Mother)

Turkey Point Light	Fannie Salter
Elk Neck River/Chesapeake Bay	1925 - 1947
	Replaced: Clarence W. Salter (Husband)

Maine:

Deer Island Thoroughfare Light	Melissa Holden
Mark Island/Penobscot Bay	1874 - 1876
	Replaced: Samuel E. Holden (Husband)

Doubling Point Range Lights	Karen McLean
Kennebec River	1986 -
	Replaced:

Monhegan Light	Betsy G. Morrow Humphrey
Monhegan Island	1862 - 1880
	Replaced: Joseph F. Humphrey (Husband)

Pond Island Light	Harriet Gill
Kennebec River Entrance	1864 - 1869
	Replaced: Sam Gill (Husband)

White Head Light	Abbie O. (Burgess) Grant
Penobscot Bay	1875 - 1892
	Replaced: Isaac Grant (Husband)

Michigan:

Bay City Light Mouth of Saginaw River	Julia Brawn 1873 - 1890 Replaced: Peter Brawn (Husband)
Beaver Island Harbor Point Light North End Lake Michigan	Elizabeth Williams 1872 - 1884 Replaced Clement Van Riper (Husband)
Bois Blanc Island Light Lake Huron	(Mrs.) Charles M. Omalley 1854 - 1855 Replaced:
Bois Blanc Island Light Lake Huron	Mary Grainger 1857 - 1857 Replaced:
Cheybogan Light Entrance to Cheybogan River	Jane F. Barr 1879 - 1880 Replaced: Jacob Barr (Husband)
Cheybogan Light Entrance to Cheybogan River	Eva Papa 1869 - Replaced:
Eagle Harbor Light Lake Superior	Mary A. Wheatley 1898 - 1905 Replaced:
Granite Island Light Lake Superior	Annie M. Carlson 1903 - 1905 Replaced:
Little Traverse Light Lake Michigan	Elizabeth Williams 1884 - 1913 Replaced:
Mamajuda Light Grosse Ile	Caroline Litigot 1874 - 1885 Replaced: Barney Litigot (Husband)
Manitou Island Light Off Keewanau Peninsula/Lake Superior	Lydia Smith 1855 - 1856 Replaced:
Marquette Light Marquette Harbor/Lake Superior	Eliza Truckey 1862 - 1865 Replaced: Nelson Truckey (Husband)
Mission Point Light Grand Traverse Bay	Sarah E. Lane 1906 - 1908 Replaced: Husband

Muskegon Light
Harbor Entrance/Lake Michigan

(Mrs.) William M. Monroe
1862 - 1871
Replaced: William Monroe (Husband)

Pentwater Light
Lake Michigan

Annie McGuire
1877 -
Replaced:

Presque Isle Range Light
Lake Huron

Anna Garraty
1903 - 1926
Replaced: Patrick Garraty (Husband)

Sand Point (Escanaba) Light
L'Anse Bay/Lake Superior

Mary Terry
1868 - 1886
Replaced: John Terry (Husband)

Squaw Point Light
Little Bay de Noc, Northern Peninsula

Kate Marvin
1898 - 1904
Replaced: Husband

St. Joseph's Light
Lake Michigan/St. Joseph River Entrance

S. B. Carlton
1861 -
Replaced: M. G. Carlton (Husband)

St. Joseph's Light
Lake Michigan

Jane Enos
1877 -
Replaced:

St. Mary's River Light

(Mrs.) Donald E. Harrison
1902 - 1904
Replaced:

Mississippi:

Biloxi Light
Gulf of Mexico

Mary J. Reynolds
1854 - 1866
Replaced:

Biloxi Light
Gulf of Mexico

Maria Younghans
1867 - 1919
Replaced: Perry Younghans (Husband)

Biloxi Light
Gulf of Mexico

Miranda Younghans
1919 - 1929
Replaced: Maria Younghans (Mother)

Pascagoula Light
East Pascagoula Bay

Celestine Dupont
1855 -
Replaced:

Pass Christian Light Mississippi Sound	C. A. Hiern 1844 - 1861 Replaced: Roger Hiern (Father)
Pass Christian Light Mississippi Sound	Alice Butterworth 1877 - Replaced:
Round Island Light Mississippi Sound	Margaret Anderson 1872 - 1881 Replaced: Charles Anderson (Husband)
Ship Island Light Gulfport Channel	Mary R. Havens 1855 - 1856 Replaced: Edward Havens (Husband)

New Jersey:

Bergen Point Light Newark Bay Entrance	Hannah McDonald 1873 - 1879 Replaced:
Passaic Light Newark Bay	Elizabeth MacCashin 1903 - 1914 Replaced: Husband

New York:

Bluff Point Light Lake Champlain	Mary J. Herwerth 1881 - 1905 Replaced: William G. Herwerth (Husband)
Cow Island Light Hudson River	(Mrs.) Thomas Hudson 1853 - Replaced:
Cumberland Head Light Lake Champlain	Emma D. Tabberah 1904 - 1919 Replaced: William H. Tabberrah (Husband)
Elm Tree Light Staten Island	Ann Hooper 1859 - 1865 Replaced: William Hooper (Husband)
Four Mile Point Light Hudson River	Annie Jerome 1863 - 1864 Replaced:
New Baltimore Light Hudson River	Eliza Smith 1864 - 1870 Replaced: James Smith (Husband)

Old Field Point Light Long Island Sound	Elizabeth Smith 1830 - 1856 Replaced: Walter Smith (Husband)
Old Field Point Light Long Island Sound	Mary A. Foster 1856 - Replaced: Elizabeth Smith
Old Field Point Light Long Island Sound	(Mrs.) Edward Shoemaker 1826 - 1827 Replaced: Edward Shoemaker (Husband)
Robbins Reef Light Staten Island/New York Harbor	Kate Walker 1894 - 1919 Replaced: John Walker (Husband)
Rondout Creek Light Hudson River	Catherine Murdock 1857 - 1907 Replaced: George Murdock (Husband)
Sampher Dock Light Beacon Hudson River	Charlotte H. Clements 1897 - 1906 Replaced:
Saugerties Light Hudson River	Kate A. Crowley 1873 - 1885 Replaced:
Schodack Channel Light Hudson River	Joanna Lawton 1860 - Replaced: Richard Lawton (Husband)
Stony Point Light Hudson River	Nancy Rose 1871 - 1904 Replaced: Alexander Rose (Husband)
Stony Point Light Hudson River	Melinda Rose 1904 - 1905 Replaced: Nancy Rose (Mother)
Stuyvesant Light Hudson River	Ann Witbeck 1853 - Replaced:
Throggs Neck Light Long Island Sound	Ellen Lyons 1876 - 1878 Replaced: Richard Lyons (Husband)

Throggs Neck Light Long Island Sound	E. Kilmartin 1878 - 1881 Replaced: Ellen Lyons

Ohio:

Marblehead Light Sandusky Bay Entrance/Lake Erie	Rachel Wolcott 1832 - 1834 Replaced: Benjamin Wolcott (Husband)
Marblehead Light Sandusky Bay Entrance/Lake Erie	Joanna H. McGee 1896 - 1903 Replaced:
Turtle Island Light Maumee Bay Entrance	Ann Edson 1869 - 1870 Replaced: Nathan Edson (Husband)

Rhode Island:

Beavertail Light Narragansett Bay Entrance	Demaris Weeden 1848 - 1857 Replaced: Robert Weeden (Husband)
Bristol Ferry Light Strait from Narragansett Bay	Elizabeth Diman 1856 - 1857 Replaced: Henry Diman (Husband)
Lime Rock Light Newport Harbor	Ida Lewis (Wilson) 1879 - 1903 Replaced: Capt. Hosea Lewis (Father)
Newport Harbor Light Goat Island/Newport Harbor Entrance	Mary Ann Heath 1868 - Replaced: John Heath (Husband)
Newport Harbor Light Goat Island/Newport Harbor Entrance	L. Crawford 1878 - Replaced: H. W. Crawford (Husband)
Watch Hill LIght Fishers Island Sound	Sally Ann Crandall 1879 - 1888 Replaced: Jared Crandall (Husband)
Watch Hill Light Fishers Island Sound	Fannie Schuyler 1888 - Replaced:

South Carolina:

Cambahee Light St. Helena Sound	Bridget Comer 1869 - Replaced:

Virginia:

Nansemond River Light
Nansemond River

Ella Edwards
1903 - 1906
Replaced: E. M. Edwards (Husband)

Old Point Comfort Light
Entrance Hampton Roads Harbor

Amelia Deweese
1857 - 1861
Replaced:

Vermont:

Windmill Point Light
Lake Champlain

Clarinda Mott
1859 - 1862
Replaced:

Washington:

Dofflemyer Point Fog Signal Station
Budd Inlet

Madeline Campbell
1965 - 1987
Replaced: Bob Robinson

Ediz Hook Light
Puget Sound

Mary Smith
1870 - 1874
Replaced: George Smith (Father)

Ediz Hook Light
Puget Sound

Laura Blach Stratton
1874 - 1885
Replaced: Mary Smith

Mukilteo Light
Point Elliott

Mrs. Christiansen
1925 - 1927
Replaced: Husband

New Dungeness Light
Strait of Juan de Fuca

Jeni Burr
1980 -
Replaced:

Semiahmoo Light
Canadian Border

Esther Durgan
1925 -
Replaced:

Wisconsin:

North Point (Milwaukee) Light
Lake Michigan

Georgia A. Stebbins
1881 - 1899
Replaced: D. K. Green (Father)

Port Washington Light
Lake Michigan

? Schooner
1860 -1861
Replaced: B. Schooner (Husband)

Sand Island Light
Apostle Islands/Lake Superior

Ella G. Quick
1903 - 1906
Replaced: Emmanuel Quick (Husband)

Source: "Lighthouse Keepers and Assistants" (handwritten): Volume I, 1828-1857; Volume II, 1851-1871; Volume III, 1853-1871, Districts 1-8; Volume IV, 1869-1880; Volume V, 1872-1880; Volume VI, 1879-1905, Districts 6-13; Volume VII (no dates). Located in Record Group 26, Entry 92, National Archives, Washington, D.C. These volumes listed 122 appointments of women as official keepers, all of whom are included in this appendix.

Some of the handwriting in these registers was very difficult to read; for example, Ellis was read as Ellie, but corrected through correspondence. Nor could first names like Darrell be easily identified as masculine or feminine, so the total may not be exact.

This appendix does not include dozens of women who served for a period of months (less than a year) after a father's or husband's death, while they waited for the arrival of a new keeper. Nor does it include the many women who served as assistant keepers, of whom over 240 names were tallied from the registers listed above. Several of the women whose careers are detailed in this book, however, served as both assistant keepers and as keepers. Two in particular--Catherine Moore and Abbie Burgess--began keeping the lights while still in their teens and spent most of their lives in lighthouses. Because their experiences as assistants in the first half of the 19th century (when documentation was generally very scanty) have been recorded, those years are included in their chapters.

The total number of official women keepers included in this appendix is 138, some of whom have been added for the period both before and after the volumes listed above were recorded.

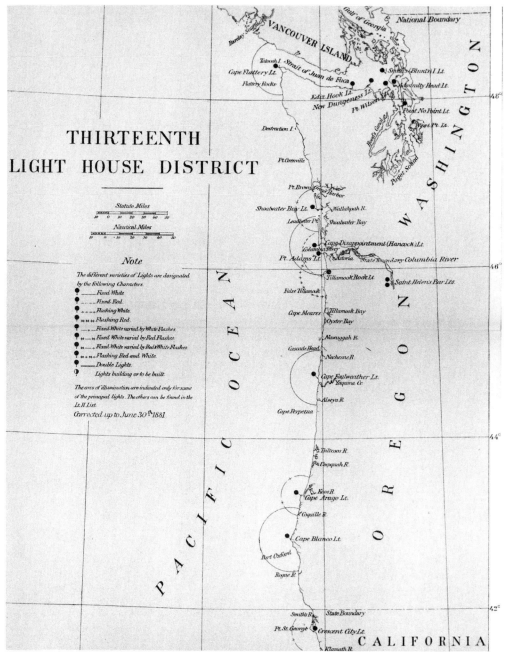

1881 Annual Report of the Lighthouse Board.

Endnotes

1. See Carol Ruth Berkin and Mary Beth Norton, *Women in America: A History* (Boston: Houghton Mifflin Co., 1979) for further information, particularly Part III: Nineteenth Century America—the Paradox of "Women's Sphere."

2. In his book *The Lighthouses of New England* the lighthouse historian Edward Rowe Snow wrote (without identifying his sources) that John Thomas was Major General John Thomas, who had a wife named Hannah and died during the Revolutionary War. The Curator of the Pilgrim Society in Plymouth, Massachusetts, maintains, however, that General Thomas was a medical man who lived and practiced in Kingston, Massachusetts, so could hardly have kept the lights on Gurnet Point. The Thomases who kept the Gurnet Point Lights were more likely another couple with the same names.

Snow also said that Hannah Thomas was still keeping the Gurnet Point Light in 1790 when it was turned over to the federal government, but Coast Guard pamphlet CG-232, *Historically Famous Lighthouses,* states that by 1786 the Gurnet Point Light was being kept by Thomas Burgess. These discrepancies are typical of the problems posed when using secondary sources to research lighthouses and their keepers.

3. The quotes in this chapter are based on an article published in the *New York Sunday World* in 1889, much of which was recorded by Ivan Justinius in his *History of Black* Rock (Bridgeport: Anoniak Printing Service, Inc., 1955) and by Pat Jordan in her essay, "The Keeper of Black Rock Light" in *The New England Sampler II* (Concord, New Hampshire: 1971). Other information comes from an article in the *Bridgeport Standard* on 25 March 1878.

4. Personal communication with Village Historian of Old Field, 1991.

5. Personal communication with Point Lookout State Park, 1991.

6. An article about the Mabrity and Bethel families at Key West Light appeared in the *Key West Citizen,* May 31, 1989.

7. Information on lighthouses on Long Island Sound is found in Harlan Hamilton, *Lights and Legends.*

8. Harlan Hamilton, *Lights and Legends.*

9. Information is taken from Robert deGast, *The Lighthouses of the Chesapeake,* and annual reports of the Lighthouse Board located in Record Group 26 at the National Archives, Washington, D.C.

10. "Lighthouses of Penobscot Bay—Mark Island," by Clayton H. Gross in *Island Ad-vantages,* March 15, 1990.

11. Twin towers permitted navigators to line up two lights and thus determine one exact location. Several decades later, more sophisticated means of determining location were developed, and twin lights were no longer needed.

12. Segments of Abbie Burgess's letters are quoted in several sources, including Ross Holland, Robert Carse, and Edward Rowe Snow.

13. For greater detail about the development of the Lighthouse Service, see Francis Ross Holland, Jr., *America's Lighthouses* (New York: Dover Publications, Inc., 1972).

14. Series E, Volume 54, Pettus.

15. This letter is included in an article entitled "Biloxi's Lady Lighthouse Keeper," by M. James Stevens in *The Journal of Mississippi History,* date unknown.

16. Much of the information in this chapter was supplied by the Curator of Historic Facilities, Tullis-Toledano Manor, Biloxi, and included mimeographed descriptions of the Biloxi Light, as well as copies of two articles about women keepers at Biloxi Light by Kat Bergeron published in the *Sun/Herald,* 4/1/84, and in the journal of the Lighthouse Preservation Society, 4/1/84. Other clippings came from the Historical Collections of the Biloxi Public Library. Technical details came from the annual reports of the Lighthouse Board.

17. Discussions of West Coast lighthouses can be found in a number of books focusing on that region, including Ralph Shanks, *Lighthouses and Lifeboat Stations of San Francisco Bay,* and *Guardians of the Golden Gate,* and Frank Perry, *Lighthouse Point: Reflections on Monterey Bay.*

18. *1902 Annual Report of the Lighthouse Board.*

19. This same story is told in "Emily Fish, the Socialite Keeper," by Clifford Gallant, *The Keeper's Log,* Spring 1985, Vol. I, No. 3, p. 10.

20. *1907 Annual Report of the Lighthouse Board.*

21. Pages 33-50.

22. Some of the information in this chapter is based on material collected by Clifford Gallant and incorporated in an article by him entitled, "Emily Fish, the Socialite Keeper," in the Spring 1985 issue of *The Keeper's Log*—the journal of the U.S. Lighthouse Society. Gallant's files, including private correspondence regarding Charlotte Layton, are at the U.S. Lighthouse Society headquarters in San Francisco. Ralph Shanks' two books contain further information.

23. This chapter is based on newspaper articles and a fact sheet supplied by the Hudson River Maritime museum in Kingston, New York.

24. *Instructions to Light-Keepers* were issued several times by the Lighthouse Board. This quote is from page 12 of the 1902 publication.

25. This chapter is based on Harriet Colfax's logs, archived in the National Archives in Suitland, Maryland; on clippings and information

sheets supplied by the curator of the Old Lighthouse Museum, Michigan City Historical Society, Inc.; and on annual reports of the Lighthouse Board. Two articles about the Michigan City Light were also useful: "Michigan City: Indiana's only Lighthouse," by Patricia Harris, appeared in the Spring 1987 issue of *The Keeper's Log*, U.S. Lighthouse Society. "A woman's place was in the lighthouse" by Susan Meyer appeared in the *USCG Commandant's Bulletin* 47-80.

26. These entries are taken from Mary Ryan's log, and were published in *The Keeper's Log*, U.S. Lighthouse Society, Spring 1991.

27. The librarian of the Santa Barbara Historical Society provided clippings about Julia Williams, as well as a copy of her son Bion's memoir and an interview with her grandson. An article about the Santa Barbara Light appeared in *The Keeper's Log*, U.S. Lighthouse Society, Winter 1993.

28. Escanaba *Iron Port,* March 6, 1886.

29. This chapter is based on material supplied by the Delta County Historical Society in Escanaba, Michigan, including an article in *The Delta Historian,* entitled "Two Women among Nine Sand Point Lighthouse Keepers," by Richard Stratton, and two clippings from 1886 issues of the Escanaba *Iron Port*. The Historical Society is in the process of restoring the Sand Point Lighthouse—taken out of service in 1938—to its original appearance.

30. *Instructions to Light-Keepers*, p. 5.

31. Clippings, a short memoir by Melinda Rose, and copies of the correspondence regarding her appointment were provided by Stony Point Battlefield personnel.

32. This chapter stems from multiple sources: a long entry on Ida Lewis in *Notable American Women* (Belknap Press of Harvard University Press, 1971); articles in U.S. Coast Guard publications; a mimeographed monograph from Coast Guard files entitled "Historical Paintings Project: Ida Lewis, Keeper of Lime Rock Lighthouse and the Rescue of Two Men on 4 February 1881," by Dennis L. Noble; and clippings from several Rhode Island newspapers, currently filed in the Coast Guard's Historian Office in Washington, D.C.

33. Elizabeth Williams, *A Child of the Sea*, p. 213.

34. Ibid., pp. 214-5.

35. Ibid., pp. 214-5. Elizabeth Williams's book, *A Child of the Sea* (privately printed by Elizabeth Whitney Williams in 1905; reprinted in 1983 by the Beaver Island Historical Society), was provided by the Beaver Island Historical Society. A short biography of Elizabeth Williams was also provided by the Michigan Women's Historical Center.

36. Annual reports of the Lighthouse Board.

37. Annie Bell Hobbs's article was reproduced in Robert Carse, *Keepers of the Lights*.

38. Information supplied by the Monhegan Historical and Cultural Museum Association.

39. *Women of Bay County, 1809-1980* (Bay City, Michigan: The Museum of the Great Lakes, 1980).

40. Private correspondence supplied by the Calvert Marine Museum.

41. From an obituary supplied by the Clinton County Historical Association.

42. Luther Barrett, "Successful Woman Lighthouse Keeper," Delta County Historical Society Newsletter (date unknown).

43. Based on an article in *The Keeper's Log,* Winter 1987, by Lenore Nicholson, entitled "Point Fermin Lighthouse—Life Long Love Affair."

44. Page 13.

45. This genealogy appears in the brochure published by the Friends of the Concord Point Lighthouse, as well as several other sources. An article in a Baltimore newspaper by Henry O'Neill's niece, Catherine O'Neill Gunther, states, however, that Esther O'Neill was the second of John O'Neill's daughters rather than his daughter-in-law. This would make her Henry's sister.

Information gathered by volunteer historical organizations is often based on secondary sources, stemming from local legend as much as from archival records. The validity of data can be very hard to verify.

46. This chapter is based on reminiscences by Caroline Curtin, Kate McDougal's granddaughter, born in 1909 at Mare Island Naval Shipyard while her grandmother was keeper of the lighthouse at the other end of Mare Island. Mrs. Curtin lives in Williamsburg, Virginia, and generously shared photos and memorabilia with the authors.

47. A few technical details in this chapter were taken from annual reports of the Lighthouse Board. A chapter about Kate McDougal, based on personal recollections of another granddaughter, also appears in Ralph Shanks, *Guardians of the Golden Gate.*

48. Page 6.

49. The Registrar of the Santa Cruz City Museum of Natural History sent an article by Frank Perry entitled "California's Lighthousekeeper Naturalist." Laura Hecox's career is also outlined in Frank Perry, *Lighthouse Point: Reflections on Monterey Bay History.*

50. See David Montgomery, *Beyond Equality: Labor and the Radical Republicans 1862-1872* (New York: Vintage Books, 1967) for further information.

51. Ibid.

52. Ibid.

53. *Instructions to Light-Keepers*, page 21.

54. *New York Times,* March 5, 1906.

55. Much of the information in this chapter comes from a feature article in the *New York Times* on Sunday, March 5, 1906, Section 3, page 7, entitled, "Kept House Nineteen Years on Robbin's Reef." Other articles about Kate Walker appeared in *The Staten Island Historian* in 1978; in *American Magazine*, Volume 100, October, 1925; and in *The Keeper's Log*, Summer 1987, in an article by Clifford Gallant entitled "Mind the Light, Katie."

56. Copies of the newspaper clippings cited above are filed among Clifford Gallant's papers at the U.S. Lighthouse Society in San Francisco.

57. This chapter is based on material generously supplied by Arthur Burdette Hillegas, son of Emma Tabberrah's daughter Rose. Dr. Hillegas, born in 1907 while his grandmother was keeper at Cumberland Head Light, now lives in New Baltimore, Michigan.

58. Quotations are from a Coast Guard press release issued in 1945.

59. Much of the above information is based on a Coast Guard press release about Fannie Salter issued in 1945, written by W. W. Wilson, Sp.2c(PR), USCGR. Some details are taken from a letter written on April 21, 1979, by Fannie Mae Salter's daughter, Olga Crouch, to Clifford Gallant of Pacific Grove, California. This letter is now in the files of the U.S. Lighthouse Society in San Francisco. The authors have also enjoyed corresponding with Olga Crouch, who still lives in North East, Maryland. Olga Salter Crouch's husband was related to Georgianna Crouch Brumfield, who kept the Turkey Point Light from 1898 until 1919.

Other articles about Fannie Salter include a piece that appeared in *The Sunday Star Pictorial Magazine,* April 20, 1947; in *The Weather Gauge* (date unknown)—an article entitled "Fannie Salter—America's Last Woman Lighthouse Keeper," by Robert O. Smith; and an obituary in the Mobile *Press Register,* 13 March 1966.

60. A detailed description of the evolution of the lighthouse service can be found in Francis Ross Holland, Jr., *America's Lighthouses.*

61. The careers in the Coast Guard of both women keepers of Washington lighthouses are outlined in Sharlene and Ted Nelson, *Umbrella Guide to Washington Lighthouses.*

62. "Preliminary Inventory of Historic Lighthouses," unpublished manuscript produced by the National Park Service National Maritime Initiative, History Division, Washington, D.C., 1992.

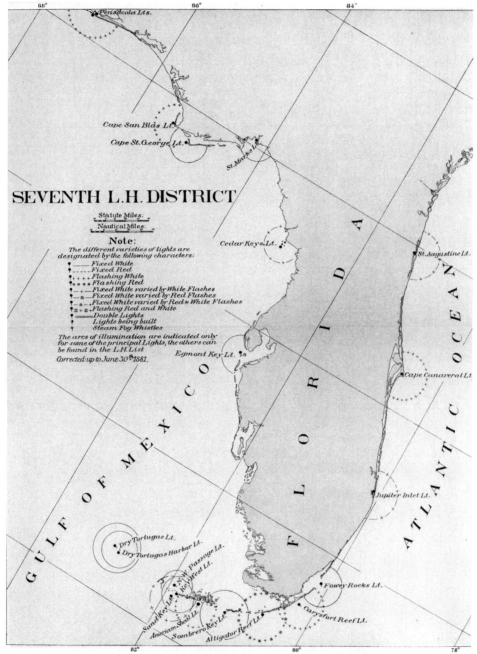

1881 Annual Report of the Lighthouse Board.

Bibliography

Anderson, Hans Christian, *Keepers of the Lights* (New York: Greenberg Publisher, 1955).

Bachand, Robert C., *Northeast Lights* (Norwalk, Connecticut: Sea Sports Publications, 1989). Specific technical and historical information on a selection of lights on the northeast coast.

Beaver, Patrick, *A History of Lighthouses* (Secaucus, New Jersey: The Citadel Press, 1973). Lighthouses all over the world. Two chapters on American lighthouses.

Carse, Robert, *Keepers of the Lights* (New York: Charles Scribner's Sons, 1969). One of the most readable of the many books about lighthouses.

deGast, Robert, *The Lighthouses of the Chesapeake* (Baltimore: Johns Hopkins University Press, 1973). Historical sketches of Chesapeake lighthouses, with numerous black-and-white photos by the author.

Gibbons, Gail, *Beacons of Light: Lighthouses* (New York: Morrow Junior Books, 1990). Basic information at an elementary school level.

Gleason, Sarah C., *Kindly Lights* (Boston: Beacon Press, 1991). A history of the lighthouses of Southern New England.

Glunt, Ruth R., *Lighthouses and Legends of the Hudson* (New York: Library Research Association, 1975).

Great Lakes Lighthouse Keepers Association, *Instructions to Light-Keepers*: A photoreproduction of the 1902 Edition of "Instructions to Light-Keepers and Masters of Light-House Vessels" (Allen Park, Michigan: Great Lakes Lighthouse Keepers Association, 1989).

Hamilton, Harlan, *Lights and Legends: A Historical Guide to Lighthouses of Long Island Sound, Fishers Island Sound, and Block Island Sound* (Stamford, Connecticut: Wescott Cove Publishing Company, 1987). A survey of both existing and former lighthouses of the area, with technical and historical information on each.

Holland, Francis Ross, *America's Lighthouses, An Illustrated History* (New York: Dover Publications, 1972). Probably the most comprehensive survey of our nation's lighthouses.

_____, *Great American Lighthouses* (Washington, DC: The Preservation Press, 1989). A guidebook to American lighthouses.

Hurley, Neil E., *Keepers of Florida Lighthouses*, 1820-1939 (Alexandria, Virginia: Historic Lighthouse Publishers, 1990).

Jones, Ray, and Bruce Roberts, *Southern Lighthouses: Chesapeake Bay to the Gulf of Mexico* (Chester, Connecticut: Globe Pequot Press, 1989).

"Lighthouse Keepers and Assistants" (handwritten): Volume I, 1828-1857; Volume II, 1851-1871; Volume III, 1853-1871, Districts 1-8; Volume IV,

1869-1880; Volume V, 1872-1880; Volume VI, 1879-1905, Districts 6-13; Volume VII (no dates). Located in Record Group 26, Entry 92, National Archives, Washington, D.C.

Lighthouse Keeper Logs, 1872-1905, National Archives, Suitland, Maryland.

National Maritime Initiative, "Preliminary Inventory of Aids to Navigation" (Washington, D.C.: National Park Service, 1993).

National Register of Historic Places, various nomination forms for lighthouses (Washington, D.C.: National Park Service).

Nelson, Sharlene P. and Ted W., *Umbrella Guide to Washington Lighthouses* (Friday Harbor, Washington: Umbrella Books, 1990).

Perry, Frank, *Lighthouse Point: Reflections on Monterey Bay History* (Soquel, California: GBH Publishing, 1982). Contains a chapter on Laura Hecox.

Putnam, George R., *Lighthouses and Lightships of the United States* (Boston and New York: Houghton Mifflin Company, 1933). Detailed description of the lighthouse service by an official who was commissioner of lighthouses for many years.

Rezmer, Joan Totten Musinski, *Women of Bay County 1809-1980* (Bay City, Michigan: The Museum of the Great Lakes, 1980).

Shanks, Ralph, *Lighthouses and Lifeboat Stations of San Francisco Bay* (San Anselmo, California: Costano Books, 1978). Contains chapters on Emily Fish at Point Pinos and Juliet Nichols at Angel Island.

_____, *Guardians of the Golden Gate* (Petaluma, California: Costano Books, 1990). Contains excellent chapters on Angel Island and Mare Island.

Small, Constance Scovill, *Lighthouse Keeper's Wife* (University of Maine Press, 1986).

Snow, Edward Rowe, *Women of the Sea* (New York: Dodd, Mead & Company, 1962).

_____, *Famous Lighthouses of America* (New York: Dodd, Mead & Company, 1955). Detailed descriptions of the construction of lighthouses, as well as the many shipwrecks associated with their locations. Contains a chapter on women who kept lights.

Stevenson, D. Alan, *The World's Lighthouses before 1820* (London: Oxford University Press, 1959). Lighthouses around the world before 1820, including a chapter on North American lighthouses before 1800.

United States Coast Guard Bicentennial Series, *The Coast Guard along the North Atlantic Coast* (Commandant's Bulletin, December 1988). Source of information about painting of Ida Lewis at Lime Rock Light.

United States Department of Transportation, *Chronology of Aids to Navigation and the Old Lighthouse Service, 1716-1939* (Washington, D.C.: Public Affairs Division, United States Coast Guard, 1974).

_____, *Historically Famous Lighthouses* (U.S. Coast Guard Public Information Division, CG-232).

_____, *Moments in History* (Washington, D.C.: U.S. Coast Guard Public Affairs Staff, 1990).

Williams, Elizabeth Whitney, *A Child of the Sea: and Life among the Mormons* (St. James, Michigan: 1905 edition reprinted by Beaver Island Historical Society, 1983).

Index

About the Authors

Mary Louise Clifford is the author of twelve books, including introductory books on Third World countries, social studies texts, and three novels. The most recent, *When the Great Canoes Came* (1993), describes the intrusion of Europeans into Virginia between 1560 and 1686 from the viewpoint of the Powhatan tribes.

J. Candace Clifford inventories maritime resources, including lighthouses, for the National Maritime Initiative, a National Park Service program which coordinates maritime preservation activities. She is coauthor of a guidebook based on an inventory of large preserved historic vessels, *Great American Ships*, published in 1992.

Ordering Information

Single copies of *Women Who Kept the Lights* are $19.95, payable to Cypress Communications, 35 E. Rosemont Ave., Alexandria, VA 22301. Price includes postage. Discounts are available for multiple copy orders. Write for more information.

Forthcoming Title in 1996

Lighthouses, Lightships, and the Gulf of Mexico, a maritime history of the Gulf of Mexico through the development of the its aids to navigation system, i.e., lighthouses and lightships, by David L. Cipra, will be available from Cypress Communications in the Fall of 1996 (ISBN 0-9636412-1-2).